Praise for LIPSTICK AND THE LEASH

"Camilla puts her finger on something no one else is talking about: how otherwise smart, organized, strong and accomplished women turn into dumb wimps with their dogs. I'm one of them! I've had dogs all my life, but Camilla is the first person who has zeroed in on the real reasons why I could not get my precious dogs to do what I ask, even though they were 'trained.'

As a movie critic I'm strong-willed, opinionated and not afraid to speak my mind, but I was a failure with my dogs. Camilla's advice changed all that. Instead of yelling, I speak more softly now and use follow-through instead of force. I make obedience fun for my dogs, instead of threatening them. I don't confuse permissiveness with love. Better communication, less emotion and the power of quiet confidence and follow-through are exactly what empowered me with my dogs and what is offered in *LIPSTICK AND THE LEASH: Dog Training a Woman's Way*. The advice in this book changed my life!"

— Jan Wahl
Dog Owner, Movie Critic, Television and Radio Personality

"Camilla's 'farm-girl' approach to a happy life with your animals struck a chord for me. Growing up, that outlook worked at both my homes — the real one and my "other" home on the Hollywood set of the Martin farm with Lassie. My own mother and my TV mom exuded the kind of quiet strength that Camilla presents as the backbone of her dog management philosophy. Somehow, she found a way to translate that heart-warming experience to paper with lively humor, creating a clever and thought-provoking book sure to be of benefit to even the wildest household!"

— Jon Provost
Timmy from "Lassie" www.jonprovost.com

"As a dog owner and a female executive in California's competitive wine industry, I can vouch for Camilla's advice on how to become more effective in training and control. Her tips on posture, eye contact and voice tone are vintage! These are the skills that finally helped me get my little terrier, Finnegan, under control at the winery and the same ones I used everyday in managing my business. Cheers to *LIPSTICK AND THE LEASH!*"

— Mary Colhoun

Former Proprietor, Landmark Vineyards – Sonoma County, CA

LIPSTICK
AND THE
LEASH

DOG TRAINING A WOMAN'S WAY

CAMILLA GRAY-NELSON

The techniques presented in this book are for informational purposes only. As each individual situation and dog are unique, you should use proper discretion, in consultation with a professional dog expert, before utilizing the information contained in this book. The author and publisher expressly disclaim responsibility for any adverse effects that may result from the use or application of the information contained in this book.

ISBN-10: 0-61546-558-7
ISBN-13: 978-0-615-46558-6
Library of Congress Control Number: 2011901478

Printed in the United States of America

First Edition

This book is dedicated to my animal mentors: Piggy the Cow, Classy the Horse and Nellie the Dog. From them, I learned that the true secrets of power and influence do not lie in fighting or force. Piggy, Classy and Nellie all got exactly what they wanted in life. They earned the respect of their peers and influenced the behavior of others while avoiding confrontation or aggression. They were my teachers of a Great Truth— that as women and human animals, our greatest power lies not in our physical strength or bravado, but in our ability to achieve our goals through calm and unwavering focus, leadership and clever influence.

I am passionate about sharing the secrets of natural power and leadership to help women (and men) get what they want from their dogs...and their lives!

Contents

Foreword

LIPSTICK AND THE LEASH: Dog Training a Woman's Way is full of tips, advice and not-so-common "common sense." Although it explains in easy steps how to create an obedient dog, this is not your typical training book. That said, I know from experience that if you build a foundation with your dog as Camilla Gray-Nelson instructs, you *will* have a good and obedient companion. Camilla understands that clarifying who leads and who follows in the relationship is the *prerequisite* for training your dog and earning his obedience. This is a book on how to foster that successful connection with your dog *naturally* so you get more of what you want from him – not through yelling or force, but through better leadership, quiet communication and learning to use "animal" energy.

As dog owners it is up to us to build relationships with our dogs that result in cooperation and good manners – dogs cannot do this alone. Trust, respect and confidence are the foundation of an obedient dog, not necessarily the commands we teach him. When someone tells me I think like a dog, I take it as a big compliment. To create a willing and obedient partner, we must think and many times act like a dog. *LIPSTICK AND THE LEASH* describes how we can do this in the simplest of terms.

Written with humor and based on real everyday experiences with dogs and people, I like it that Camilla is not afraid to talk about all topics – whether or not they are "politically correct" – in order to present a comprehensive, balanced and humane approach to dog ownership and training.

What I like most is that *LIPSTICK AND THE LEASH* is easy to read and easy to understand. Camilla helps us relate to the dog world by pointing out similarities to many things that we have experienced in our human world. She identifies what is *dog* and what is *human* in each of our mannerisms and ways. More importantly, she explains why conflicts can occur between our two species (even though we do not mean to create them), and how we can minimize these conflicts by thinking and communicating more like a dog.

Men always believe they are good dog trainers. In all my years of training I would like a dollar for the times the man in the family tells me the dog is good with him but his wife spoils the dog and cannot get the dog to do anything for her. Though the man of the house is rarely perfect or without blame for the dog's bad behaviors, it is often the woman in the home who is left with the responsibility of "fixing" the dog and creating the perfect family companion. This book is a valuable resource on how she can achieve that.

Even though Camilla wrote this book for women, I recommend and hope that men will read it and apply what they read to their own relationships with their dogs. More than a few men are macho on the outside but mush on the inside with their best friend.

LIPSTICK AND THE LEASH helps all of us understand how to communicate more effectively with our canine partners, build rich relationships with them and create memories that will last a lifetime.

— Martin Deeley
2011 Hall of Fame inductee, International Association of Canine Professionals

Introduction

I've come to believe that each of us has a personal calling that's as unique as a fingerprint—and that the best way to succeed is to discover what you love and then find a way to offer it to others in the form of service.
—*Oprah Winfrey*

"Stand up straight, dear." "Don't mumble." "No one finds that frown attractive." "Be a lady and stick to your principles." My mother's words still ring in my ears. Through my childhood, teens, and college years, her advice and her role model of grace, kindness and quiet strength were instrumental in preparing me for an effective and successful life. I had no idea, however, that her advice was also preparing me to be a dog trainer!

The animals on our farm were also my teachers. In their own way, they taught me the true nature of power and influence. The Queen of the Herd, the Lead Horse, and the Top Dog all got there without serious fighting or confrontation. Instead they used body language, boundaries, focus, and quiet determination to achieve and hold their positions of power. *Had my mother been talking to them, too?*

When I started my dog-training business well over twenty years ago, I did house calls. It was usually women who sought my help because they were being overwhelmed by the family dog. They were either angry and yelling or being overly permissive and smothering, both of which made them ineffectual, and the dogs ran their lives. Because these were house calls, *I also got to observe their kids.* Invariably, the women that could not control their dogs could not control their children either.

Something started to click in my brain. The very skills these women needed to control their dogs were the *same* ones they needed to control their children...and probably other parts of their lives as well.

- Don't yell; stay calm.
- Set boundaries and then enforce them. If you don't set your boundaries, no one respects you—not your peers, your kids, or your dog.

- Be a *leader*, not a friend, a follower or a doormat.
- Achieve your power through *control*, not confrontation. (Fights and confrontation in the animal world are the exception, not the rule.)
- Be *effective*, not loud. (The dog doing the barking and the woman doing the yelling are not powerful or effective; the leaders are the quiet ones that simply get the job done.)

Because the vast majority of the dog-owning families leave dog responsibilities to us women, literally *thousands* of you have come to me over the years—feeling powerless, frustrated and defeated. You assume that dog training requires either masculine strength and bravado (which you do not possess) or endless cookies and treats (which you are reluctant to use or that have not solved your issues.) You are desperate for help.

I am passionate about helping women and saving dogs. If you have a dog that seems beyond control, don't give up! Your dog is not impossible; he's just confused because you are not communicating in his language. He ignores your frustration and yelling because he sees it as weakness, not strength. Learn the secrets of calm, effective power and leadership, and you will be amazed at the turnaround in your dog. Try it on your kids, your husband and your coworkers while you're at it!

What makes *Lipstick and the Leash* special is that it points out the profound parallels between canine behavior and that of human beings. *We are all connected!* The nature of power, how it is achieved quietly, and how clever leadership uses that power to influence (not force) the behavior of others is the real message of *Lipstick and the Leash*. Dog training becomes a metaphor for life!

By focusing on a woman's special challenges in dog training and developing her hidden strengths, *Lipstick and the Leash* can help *you* discover your Inner Leader, train a dog that will make you and your family proud, and ultimately give you a road map for getting more of what you want in life.

Enjoy.

❖ Part I ❖
There Ain't No Lassie, Lassie!

An Honest Look At Real Dogs

1
If You Fall in the Well, I Hope You Can Swim

*Hollywood and Television Have Warped Our Perception
of Dogs and Created "The Lassie Syndrome"*

Yesterday I was a dog.
Today I'm a dog.
Tomorrow, I'll probably still be a dog.
There's just so little hope for advancement.
—Charles Schultz

Lassie, Rin Tin Tin, Clifford the Big Red Dog and count-less others through the years – they have been smart, kind, dependable and human-like...*yet none of them real.* Did you know that Lassie was not a girl at all, but a boy—several of them? Or that Rin Tin Tin, the heroic German Shepard on screen, is said to have regularly bit-ten his handler off-camera, causing many filming delays? Movies, Saturday morning cartoons and most fiction writ-ers have painted for us a picture of dogs that, in most cas-es, reflects what we *want* dogs to be, rather than a true depiction of the animals they are. Unfortunately, these fictional portrayals of dogs color our real-life perceptions, often with devastating consequences. Most of us have grown up *believing* that dogs are gentle creatures that live to please and serve their masters, and would sacri-fice their own lives to save ours. It's a beautiful fantasy, but as with most fantasies, it just ain't so. Even the stories of dogs "saving" their families from burning buildings, de-tecting cancer or predicting seizures are written through the rose-colored glasses of the authors, who themselves may not realize that even in these cases, dogs are acting more on instinct than altruism.

Myths Debunked and the Lassie Syndrome

We have a lot of ideas and beliefs about dogs. Many of them come from movies we've seen and the stories we've read about dogs. Even television specials about dogs are produced for the "ahhhh factor," whether they are about dogs helping the disabled or a dog whose barking alerts his family to a fire in their home and saves their lives. Unfortunately, those movies, books and TV specials are written to entertain us and make us feel all warm and fuzzy—not to educate us about real dogs. And it's not just major media. Local news stories are often written through the perspective of reporters who believe what they've heard and read about dogs through the years. Dog bite incidents that make the news are seen as freak accidents, and the dogs involved are considered "bad." The fact is that dogs are animals. Even owning a pet dog does not give you a true view of dogs in their natural state. *The result is that many of us believe and expect dogs to be something they're not.* Do any of the following statements sound true to *you*?

1. Dogs are born with a desire to please their masters.
2. A dog will protect his family because he loves them.
3. A dog will not hurt someone he loves.
4. Puppies eventually grow out of bad behavior or you just love them through it.

Some dog experts refer to this as "The Lassie Syndrome," a series of myths that revolve around what we *want* to believe about dogs and which have been bolstered and institutionalized through popular culture. I'm sorry to have to do this, but for our own sake and that of our dogs, let me bust these myths one by one.

Myth #1: Dogs are born with a desire to please their masters.

Ha! First and foremost, dogs are born with a desire to please *themselves*, not their masters. A dog will protect himself and his territory before he'll protect his family, because as an animal of Nature, *his survival* is his most important instinct, not bringing a smile to his master's face. Think about it. A species would not long survive by putting another's well being ahead of its own. When our dog does something for us and we praise him for it, pet him or give him a treat, it's not the *serving us* that pleases him—it's the praise or the petting or the cookie that we give him! Your dog actually doesn't give a fig about how you feel about his behavior, beyond how you make *him* feel about it. How many times have you yelled at your dog to stay out of the garbage or expressed your displeasure about his chasing the cat? He's still doing it, isn't he? *Dogs are about pleasure, not pleasing.* If it's fun for them, they'll do it. How *you* feel about it is immaterial. Again, my apologies. Don't shoot the messenger. My point is simply this: when we expect our dog to want to please us but he doesn't seem to care, we are disappointed. We are not as happy with our dog. We are frustrated and confused by him. We are expecting our dog to live up to a standard that he can never achieve, because it is *not* in his DNA. How unfair is that?

Myth #2: A dog will protect his family because he loves them.

As a card-carrying creature of Nature, a dog's priority is to protect himself, not others. Protection of self, of territory and of possessions or resources is foremost to a dog—not necessarily the protection of his human family. Now, if a dog's family happens to be in his territory when it is threatened and he is defending it for himself, that's his family's good luck!

One of my favorite musical questions, so eloquently asked by the incomparable Tina Turner is, "What's love got to do with it?" Love has nothing to do with it when it comes to dogs! Their actions are motivated by self-preservation, not love. "Oh, say it isn't so!" you exclaim. "Does this mean my dog doesn't love me?" Not at all. It's clear to me that dogs do feel love as an emotion, and that they really do love us, their human pack-mates. Every dog owner knows the utter joy of a dog's adoration and loving companionship. Heck. Only love could have caused humans and dogs to forge a relationship so unlikely, yet so epic, so undeniable and so permanent. Love your dog, and revel in his, but don't expect him to be obedient or gallant as part of the deal.

Myth #3: A dog will not hurt someone he loves.

Don't accept your dog's admiration as
conclusive evidence that you are wonderful.
—Ann Landers

Dogs react before they reason. If you believe that a dog will not hurt someone he loves...just try to take a fresh bone away from him when he's really into it. Dogs are instinctive, not intellectual. If I see one more mother send her toddler running toward me to "pet the nice doggie coming on the leash" as I'm out walking a client's dog, I'll scream. *Dogs aren't Lassie, woman!* Even if I'm walking one of my own dogs, I step between them. They would probably react calmly to such charging Mini-me's, but there are equal odds that they wouldn't. A family dog can love the new baby, but if the baby crawls up to his bowl while he's eating, all bets are off in the biting department. Just check the dog bite statistics. My dogs love me, but I proceed with caution if I need to take away something they have locked in their jaws and are guarding it as if it were the Ark of the Covenant itself.

These are dogs, after all. They love us, but as I asked before, what's love got to do with it? Lassie might share her bone with me and ask me what else I wanted. A *real* dog would more likely bite to save the bone he had, and then hoard all the rest of them in the house. Later, he'd lie on the floor with me, watch TV, share popcorn and cuddles...until I got up and accidentally stepped on his tail. In that moment of pain, he'd most likely bite me. Ah, dogs.

You can see the potentially dangerous disconnect here. Many children as well as adults are bitten by dogs that "love" them because they assumed it couldn't or wouldn't happen. Guess again.

Myth #4: Puppies eventually grow out of bad behavior or you just love them through it.

Puppies don't grow out of bad behavior; the bad behavior just gets bigger with the dog until he's too old and too tired to try it anymore! Now if we're talking chewing, teething and anything else related to a developmental stage, puppies will and do grow out of that behavior. Personality, however, and the behaviors that result are another matter. Puppies don't "grow out" of their personalities any more than we humans do. A confident puppy will be a confident dog, barring any unforeseen trauma. Having only my own observations (though not statistics), I am consistently amazed to see that—even raised in horrific circumstances—a confident puppy more often than not will develop into a confident adult dog. A timid puppy, on the other hand, will be a timid dog, even with the best of upbringings, *including* extensive "socialization." Personality is one of the most reliable predictors in nature. *Genes win out and instinct always prevails over training.* And you can quote me on that!

I often describe puppies and their personalities as icebergs. The personality of every dog is there at birth, but when they are puppies, we only see the tip of the iceberg. With age, the iceberg rises, until age three or so, when the full personality has developed, the iceberg is then fully exposed and visible for all to see. The early hints of personality and resulting behavioral traits that we see in a young puppy are *just the beginning* of what we will see in him as an adult dog. Not knowing this, many an unsuspecting dog owner will pick a puppy with behavioral traits they assume will "go away with age," or that they can "train out of him." The Lassie Syndrome and its inherent myths have set them up for disappointment and/or failure. Most of my business, as a dog trainer and behavior consultant, is the result of Lassie Syndrome fallout: when myth and reality collide.

2
You Smell Like a Girl...Out of My Way!

A Look into the Canine Culture of Hierarchy and Power, and Why Women Are Often at a Natural Disadvantage

It's a Man's World—Even if You're a Dog

Growing up in the age of the Women's Movement, it pains me to say this but here goes: *most of nature really is male dominated and male oriented.* A look at most of your social-group mammals like horses, cows and dogs reveals that in large groups, a male consistently holds the top power position. In a dog pack, we refer to the top dog as the Alpha dog. The Alpha dog is always a male—not because he is a macho pig, but because *breeding rights* to all the females in the group is what goes along with being the Alpha dog. This is Nature's way of assuring that only the strongest genes are passed along in the greatest numbers to subsequent generations, thereby giving that species the greatest chance for long-term survival. Well, if we put it that way...I guess I'm not quite as offended by the whole idea. And it's important going forward, ladies, that we not hold grudges against our dogs for this fact of nature. Female dogs play important roles in their species' society, but they are, for the most part, supporting roles: mothers, middle management, department heads, maybe cabinet posts... but never President.

How the Pack is Organized—The Man's on Top...Again!

The power hierarchy of social mammals is often described as a "ladder" with ascending rungs bottom to top indicating the relative power of each group member, one to another. In a classic group hierarchy of animals in the wild there are often separate power ladders for male and female members, but a supreme Alpha resides at the top, with power over all. Whether we are talking wolves, dogs, sheep, cows or horses, *this Alpha figure is always male.* It will be a bull, a stallion, a ram or some other rendition of an Alpha Male. There

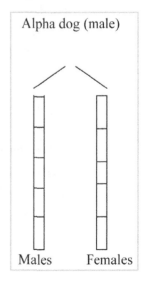

Alpha dog (male)

Males   Females

is a practical reason for this, as a strong male leader has *traditionally* meant survival of the group, assuring healthy and plentiful offspring as well as protection and ownership of territory and the food sources on it.

In our domestic world, these separate, non-competing power ladders for the other males and females may explain why it's easier and creates less conflict to introduce a new dog of a *different* sex to the dog that already calls your house home. It would make sense, since in traditional canine culture, males and females did not need to compete for the power positions in the family– their hierarchy ladders were separate. The fact that the supreme Alpha Dog was traditionally a big, strong male, however, is at the core of why women struggle to be taken seriously today as they attempt to control the dogs in their family. The supreme leader they are expecting is big and strong...and women generally are neither. In other words, women start out with two strikes against them in Nature's power game.

Hierarchy in the Modern Dog World

A lot has been said lately about the "new science" of dog behavior. It concludes that pet dogs of today have evolved to a point where hierarchy and status no longer matter to them. The greater implication, of course, is that trying to "outrank" or be socially superior to your dog in training is somehow obsolete today or worse -- inhumane. This seemed so contrary to what I know to be true about animals from my own life experience. I ran right out and bought the newest books on the shelf.

In reading them, two major premises confused me even more: #1) That hierarchy is determined through aggression and violence. #2) That outranking your dog involves intimidation, fear and pain. No wonder the conclusions don't make sense. *They are based on faulty assumptions!* Hierarchy is not and never has been about aggression or violence and it rarely involves fear or pain.

Apparently, the authors were never raised on a farm where hierarchy in its purest form is daily on display.

While few dogs today live in wild familial packs, they still live in social groups. A "pack" for today's dog, however, is the family with whom he lives or the dogs with whom he plays. It is a multi-cultural *micro-pack* if you will, made up of human adults and kids, canines, and maybe the occasional feline thrown in for good measure. Sometimes it's the *ad hoc* pack at doggie daycare or at the local dog park.

Changing the appearance of the traditional dog pack does not change the nature of its members, however. Dogs still yearn for organizational clarity, *as do humans* -- the most "evolved" animal of all. Leaders and followers will still emerge because it is Nature's timeless recipe for peace and survival. Nature is never "obsolete".

Hierarchy for today's dog is *situational*. Because dogs no longer live in large packs, the classic power ladder no longer applies. But in their interactions with members of their micro-packs, dogs do make decisions every day based on hierarchy. Maleness still matters. The age-old question, *Who wins?*, is still asked. The "winner" is the dog that best uses the time-tested, subtle signals of power to win a situational challenge, reserving physical confrontation for the rare occasion. When two dogs want the same toy, the more dominant of the two will end up with it by posturing or growling. A subordinate dog will defer and share the sofa with a human, but a dog who considers himself superior may growl to get a family member to back off. Situational hierarchy is in play all day, every day. It determines who gets the toy, who owns the sofa, whether or not your dog will allow you to trim his nails ... *and who obeys whom.*

No "Equality" in the Dog World!

One rule that is consistent, whether two ladders or one, is that there is no sharing of rungs on any power ladder! Equality, if you will, is a non-concept in the dog world. If you're a dog, you either rank higher than your fellow dog or are subordinate to him or her. You are not equals. Period. End of story. Nada mas. If you are one of those dog owners that harbor the notion that you and your dog are buddies or equals...rest assured your dog has other ideas! Let me illustrate:

Have you ever owned more than one dog at a time, and given them each a bone or toy, "to be fair"? What happened? You probably looked around several minutes later, only to find that one dog had them all. It's because there is no "sharing" in the dog world. No "fairness." No "equality." The top dog in any group gets all the stuff. That's how it works. Remember the alpha dog that has breeding rights to all of the females? I rest my case.

I'm veering a little off track, but what I'm getting at here is that if you see yourself as your dog's *equal*, he most likely sees himself as your *superior*. Somebody has to lead, and if you're not, he will. It gets even more complicated if you're a woman and you are trying to be equals with your male dog. Talk about lost in translation!

DOGS 101—A Primer

Here's my primer on dogs, and what I know to be true about them from my life experience:

- First and foremost, dogs are *animals* that just happen to live with humans. We domesticated dogs, not because we wanted a companion but because we needed their skills of hunting, killing and defense to help us humans survive and prosper.
- Selective breeding has changed the "wrapping," but not the contents. Domesticated dogs—be they toy or giant, sporting or non-sporting, long-haired or short—are still at their core, *dogs*, with remnants of all their original canine instincts, drives and social language.
- Dogs live by instincts, not by intellect. They are reactive, not thoughtful.
- Puppies are taught canine language (Dogtalk) by their mothers prior to weaning. Mother dogs initially restrain their pups with their mouths or paws. As the puppies mature, their mothers will growl, lip-curl, bark, and even nip their pups to set behavior limits. The puppies, in turn, come to understand this canine

social language before they venture out into the greater dog world.

- Adult dogs set limits among themselves by restraining, barking, bumping, and nipping. Humans are able to communicate with them in this same language through *training tools* that mimic restraint, barks, nips, and bumps.

- Dogs do *not* make responsible independent decisions because they were not designed to live independently. Dogs are programmed to do best in social groups—whether it be a familial dog pack in the wild or a human family. As social group animals, dogs depend on the direction of others to shape and limit their behaviors. *Dogs need a manager!*

- A dog will follow and obey a "strong" human but run away from a weak one. The instinct to survive attracts a dog to strength and repels him from weakness. If he is hanging out with a stronger dog, he is less likely to be picked off by the mountain lion. If he follows a weak, slow or stupid dog down the path, that dog will be the mountain lion's lunch and he will be dessert. *This attraction to strength and distain for weakness transfers to the canine-human relationship.*

- Strength—both physical and psychological—determines status in the group. Because status is a product of intelligence as well as physical ability, it is determined *not* by confrontation and brute force, but by the *ability to stop others from doing things*. The dog that can successfully stop another from doing something he does not like *has status*, whether or not he is physically big and strong.

- The "Alpha" or top dog earned that position by being able to stop *any* dog he chooses from doing *anything* he doesn't like. Status is again achieved through control (disallowing behaviors), not necessarily confrontation. *Ultimate status is the result of ultimate control.*

- Dogs avoid confrontation whenever possible. Instead, they use symbolic gestures of power (posturing, growling, barking, alpha-rolls) to gain status and control through psychological means. This usually gets the job done!

- Dogs take orders from *only* those with higher status than themselves; they ignore those of lower status.

- Dogs gravitate toward pleasure and work to avoid anything *un*pleasant. This is why a dog of status can bark or nip to stop an unwanted behavior, instead of fighting. The dog on the receiving end finds barks and nips to be unpleasant consequences and willingly ceases the behavior.
- Throughout canine history, a strong leader and a clearly established hierarchy helped ensure a pack's survival. Though they now live in our modern world, dogs are still dogs – looking for leadership and comforted by it. Having boundaries established and unwanted behaviors disallowed is still an integral part of their canine social culture, whether the "pack" is a playgroup at doggie daycare or a single dog living with a human. Times may have changed, but dogs have not; they still do best with clear rules and a strong leader.

How Positions on the Power Ladders are Determined

Contrary to popular belief, positions of power and hierarchy are *not* generally determined through conflict. "What?" you say. "But that's what they show on television!" Unfortunately, what you see on a television nature show is, at best, a one percent snapshot of Nature's big picture and how she works. The other ninety-nine percent is too *boring* to televise. When you get right down to it, television is more about ratings than education. And that's OK, as long as we recognize that television is not reality. It's the other ninety-nine percent of dog life and culture, however—the part that's *not* shown on television—that reveals how hierarchy is *really* determined between dogs.

Ignore the Weak and Follow the Strong

The average dog in a canine group occupies a rung on the power ladder that is neither at the top nor at the bottom. There are usually multiple dogs that outrank him or her, and multiple dogs that he or she outranks. *Having multiple bosses does not confuse a dog;* neither does having multiple subordinates. Dogs simply live by this credo: ignore your subordinates and follow your superiors. It is an interesting application of the dog's survival instinct at work. Subordinates are usually such because they are slower, weaker, not as smart, etc.—in other words, good targets for a predator who wants to pick off an easy meal. Anyone hanging around with those types is setting himself up to be dessert. Superiors, on the other hand, are such because they are stronger, faster and smarter. Hang around them and follow their lead, and you are more likely to survive.

The beauty of this truth is that dogs *will* obey and listen to *any* member of their pack (or family) that *outranks* them—regardless of whether he or she is absolute top dog or not. Thank goodness! We don't have to be *men*

to get our dogs to listen; we just need to "outrank" our dogs. And that, girlfriends, we accomplish by simply saying, "Don't do that," in a language our dogs can understand and respect.

The Power of "Don't Do That"—How Hierarchies Are Determined and Why Women Are at a Natural Disadvantage

Clear order in social groups keeps the group running smoothly. That's why hierarchy exists and why animals strive to figure it out. Whether it's the cows in the herd, the horses in the field, or the dogs at my boarding facility, everyday decisions re: who's on top of the hierarchy ladder, who's on the bottom, and who's in the middle happen *without* bloodshed, pain or conflict the vast majority of the time. How do they do it? Three little words: *"Don't do that."*

Rather than using physical conflict to sort out positions on the hierarchal power ladder, dogs use control. More specifically, one dog uses his ability to *stop* the behavior of another in the process of *sorting out* hierarchal order. What's more, a dog's relative position on the power ladder is determined solely by how many dogs he can stop, and how many dogs he can't. For example, if a dog in a pack of thirteen can stop or control the behavior of six of his pack mates, but the other six tell *him* what he cannot do—he is on the *middle* rung of the power ladder. This holds true for males and females, whether they are observing parallel power ladders or just one.

The dog that can stop *any* dog from doing anything he doesn't like is, by default, the top dog, or "Alpha," with a capital A. This Alpha dog is able to control or stop *all* other dogs, male or female, because of his superior size, strength and bravado. In the wilds of Nature, this would always be an intact male. In your home, a mixed species group of canines and humans, it will be the smartest, most clever and determined member of your group. For practical and safety reasons, it needs to be a human. If there is a tall, adult male human in your household, you probably see that your dogs tend to give him more respect, while you struggle. I agree that it's frustrating, but it really is nothing personal or sexist. It's just that dogs are programmed to respect size and strength. Don't get angry or frustrated. Even though, as a woman, you start out at a natural disadvantage as far as the animal world is concerned, you *can* control your dog, even if you are not male or the top dog in the family. *The secret is outranking your dog on a non-physical playing field and using your natural feminine strengths to do so.*

❖ Part II ❖
Ladies, Labs And Leadership

What Dogs Can Teach Women
About Power And Influence

3
Body Language: Your Lips Say "No," But Your Eyes Say "Yes"

Make Sure Your Body Language Is Saying What You Mean!

I speak two languages: Body and English
—Mae West

Lost in Translation

As a young woman, my girlfriend Babs traveled through Italy. She was tall and strikingly beautiful, with long, Titian blond hair and a gorgeous figure...so who needs to know the language, right? Anyway...one day, in her dismal Italian, she asked a gentleman for directions to a nearby town—at least that's what she *thought* she had asked. When he called over all the men in the village and asked her to repeat her question, their faces told Babs that she had asked for something quite different, *indeed*. Simple directions had turned into sexual innuendo. An awkward moment.

Body language is your Italian! It is the language of dogs, and they are reading every turn of your head and stoop of your shoulders throughout the day. Your body is speaking even when your lips are silent. When you give a verbal command to your dog, it's your non-verbal body language that the dog reads first. If the two are at odds, communication can fail.

Fie, fie upon her!
There's a language in her eye, her cheek, her lip.
Nay, her foot speaks; her wanton spirit looks out
at every joint and motive of her body.
—William Shakespeare

Size Matters

Have you ever watched the dogs at a dog park when a new member joins the group? There is a lot of posturing going on as members of the group re-sort and clarify their social positions—like a Friday night at the latest "in" bar in town. The "top dogs" (and those that want to be) puff themselves up and try to look as tall and important as possible. (I know a few people like that, don't you?) Dogs will even walk on their tippy-toes to gain a height advantage. If they sold shoes with lifts in the heels for dogs, I know there'd be a market for them!

Like their human counterparts, dogs want to communicate the message *"I'm important."* By standing as tall as they can, they are saying to their pack mates, *"I am more powerful than you, because I am taller and bigger."* A dog engaged in this silent conversation will stiffen his front legs and raise his neck and head, or he will move in close and hold his head above a smaller dog's, hoping the other dog will lower his head or, better yet, roll on his back and pee on himself. Ah, the ultimate concession speech! Now this, I must admit, I have never witnessed at the local bar. Humans, it seems, have developed more subtle ways of communicating subordination. "Yes, ma'am" and "As you wish, sir," have taken the place of wetting ourselves—thank goodness!

Dog's on His Throne. All's Right with the World

Why do dogs spend so much time worrying about rank? It's because a clear power hierarchy produces *peace within the group.* When each member of the group accepts his or her position and embraces it, things click along nicely: one dog on every rung of the power ladder. If everyone wanted to be the boss, there would be constant turmoil and competition. Happily, not all dogs want to be in charge. Too much pressure in the canine penthouse! Most dogs are happy to go with the flow, somewhere in the middle. Even the low dog on the totem pole does not begrudge his position. He doesn't mind working in the canine mailroom. No pressure of responsibility. Predictable. I had a cousin like that. Her favorite job as a young woman was working on the assembly line at a shoe factory. She found it relaxing and stress-free. I, on the other hand, would go crazy in such a job. I like being in control, making things happen...telling others what to do. An Alpha Bitch by birthright, that's me! Is it any surprise I became a dog trainer? Ha!

Some dogs are like me; they desire to be in charge. Someone has to be, so Nature drives *them* to fill the leadership vacuum. But Nature is also careful to produce dogs in a full range of personality types from bold to fearful, so that each can gravitate to his or her most comfortable rung on the remainder of the power ladder. Just consider for a moment how amazing that is. There is a *reason* behind your dog's personality that most likely has nothing to do with how he was raised or where he came from. There is nothing "wrong" with your fearful dog; from Nature's perspective, he is a perfect part of her grand design. Profound...but I digress.

Because different ranks within the group perform different tasks, a clear rank order also makes a dog pack more efficient. Rank is good. Rank is necessary. This is why clear rank and order put a dog at peace. I am fond of saying that dogs just want to know two things:

1. Who's driving the bus?
2. What's my seat assignment?

Answer that question adequately for your dog and watch how he settles down. The predictability and clarity of it all comforts and relaxes him. Personally, I love riding as a passenger in a car, to and from events. I leave the driving to my husband. I kick off my shoes, recline my seat and enjoy a little snooze, knowing he is at the wheel and knows the way. He's driving my bus and I have my seat assignment. All is good.

I see so many dogs in my business that owners describe as "hyper" or "overactive." These dogs are hard to live with because they never seem to settle in and relax. They jump, bark, pull on the leash, bounce off the walls and generally ignore commands. And yet, after just several minutes with me quietly yet clearly taking charge and communicating what I expect of them—a miraculous transformation occurs. The dog is calm, polite and relaxed. Owners are gobsmacked and incredulous. They can't believe it's the same dog that arrived as a whirling dervish just minutes earlier. I explain that I simply showed the dog that I was driving the bus, and that his seat assignment was somewhere behind me—not fighting over the steering wheel.

A Dog's Credo

Dogs live by two simple rules:
1. Obey superiors and ignore subordinates.
2. If it isn't fun, don't do it—no matter *who* is asking.

Does your dog ignore you? Does he only do what you ask when there's nothing else more fun or exciting? That behavior indicates that he sees you as subordinate to himself—and he's distancing himself from you because of it. It's nothing personal; it's just his survival instinct kicking in. Don't get mad. *Get rank.*

To Control, We Must Outrank...but *Quietly*

Can't we just wear the T-shirt that proudly states: "I'm My Dog's Boss"? No. Unfortunately, dogs can't read. Their understanding comes from life experience. Our dog will only *believe* that we outrank him on the power ladder if he actually experiences our control firsthand. So how *do* we communicate power and control without yelling or force? *It begins with body language.*

Using Body Language to Your Advantage

Stooped Shoulders

Daily, I see dog owners bending over to talk into their dog's face as they give a command. Are their dogs hard of hearing? Do their dogs' eyes need to engage before their ears will work? Judging from how fast a dog comes running from the other room at the slightest sound of a can opener or the crinkle of a dog treat bag, I don't think so. Their ears work just fine!

Look at this photo:

MY BODY TAKES THE SHAPE OF A "QUESTION MARK" WHEN I STOOP TO GIVE A COMMAND.

I am stooping to give the dog the command to "Down." Look carefully. My body has taken the shape of a *question mark!* It's no wonder that the dog is left thinking: *This person's not sure of what she's doing. If she's not sure of herself, why should I obey her?* The dog obviously has no intention of lying down, and is looking at me with an "Are you serious?" expression. When you stoop, you look uncertain. Even if you *are* uncertain, pretend that you're not! Stand upright and tall anyway. Fake it till you make it, I always say!

Standing Tall

THE DOMINANT DOG STANDS TALL, TO COMMUNICATE HIS POWER. THE OTHER DOG LIES DOWN TO COMMUNICATE THAT HE UNDERSTANDS AND ACCEPTS.

WHEN I STAND TALL TO GIVE THE DOWN COMMAND, I AM COMMUNICATING MY OWN POWER.

An erect posture communicates confidence. Why else would your mother have nagged you constantly to "Stand up straight!", "Watch your posture!" and "Don't slouch!"? Dogs know what Mom knew: that good posture communicates confidence, while poor posture conveys nervousness, timidity and other less than admirable personal qualities.

Dogs in a pack use posture to communicate their own power. The largest, tallest male dog is quite often boss. Standing tall when we are asking our dog to do something for us immediately communicates our message with more authority. We are quietly communicating our power. There is no need to yell or speak harshly; *the power is in the posture*. Notice the dog in the photo with me—when I stood tall, he immediately responded to my Down command.

The Play Bow Bend

Now that I've made a case for standing tall, I'll confuse you by saying that, in some instances, stooping over is a *good* thing. Let me clarify. In those instances where you are asking your dog to come *toward* you from a distance, bending from the waist can send a "come over here" message. Here's how:

Again, I'll reference back to the dog world and how dogs communicate between each other. When one dog wants another to approach and engage in play activity, he will assume what is called a "play bow." He lowers his torso, extends his front legs and may even give a playful bark. Everything about his overall demeanor is friendly and happy. Other dogs understand this invitation and happily approach him to engage.

DANE PLAY-BOWING
TO THE DOBERMAN
IN A PROMISE OF FUN

We can assume our *own* version of a play bow! When we bend forward at the waist toward our dog, extend our arms and clap our hands with happy energy—the body language message to the dog is: *come over to me and we'll have tons of fun!* It doesn't take a rocket scientist to figure out that assuming this play bow position can help us get results when we are calling our dogs to "Come!" Clapping our hands gives the dog an enticing, active "target," and the joyfulness in our voice can be irresistible. To rephrase the old Cyndi Lauper song about girls, "Dogs just want to have fu-un!" I'll talk about other modifications of the play bow bend and when to use them in my chapter on training.

I AM BENDING FORWARD IN MY OWN PLAY BOW AND PROMISE OF FUN.

I USE THE PLAY BOW BEND TO ENTICE MY DOG TO COME ON COMMAND, PROMISING A FUN AND PLEASANT RESULT!

Getting There First

When you walk your dog, which of you leads your parade? Whose body is in front and who takes up the rear? Human culture and dog culture are full of symbolic references relating to *who's in front*. The grand marshal of a parade is the *leading* car. The master of the hounds in the red coat *leads* the foxhunt, and it is considered a faux pas of the highest order to pass him. In some cultures, the man walks *in front* and, in a sign of subservience, the woman follows several paces behind. In the dog world the phrase "leader of the pack" means just that. Sit and watch a group of dogs at your local dog park and see what plays out when a ball is thrown. The strongest, most pushy, dominant dog will get to that ball first. He'll make sure he's the one in front—barking, nipping and body slamming his competitors back out of his way. Between dogs, who gets there first *matters*.

If you are able to maintain lead position during your dog walks, or at least keep your dog at your side, you will be communicating that *you* are the one with more power. The longer I train dogs to be obedient, the more I realize that the answers lie in the simple things. Something as simple as where a dog is allowed to walk while on leash with me can fundamentally begin to transform a difficult dog.

Who's in Front?

IN EVERY PHOTO, NOTICE THAT THE BORDER COLLIE IS
IN FRONT, THE DOBERMAN IN THE MIDDLE, AND THE
NEWFOUNDLAND AT THE BACK. THEY ARE HONORING AND
DEMONSTRATING THE POWER LADDER OF THEIR GROUP.

The Border Collie in these photos is clearly Queen of the Dog Park! She is in lead position in every photo! What's more, the same dog is in second position and in third bringing up the rear. Each dog secured its position in the power lineup by disallowing another from overtaking or passing him. The Border Collie nipped the Doberman and the Newfie when one or the other tried to pass her and take over her lead. The Doberman, in turn, nipped at the Newfie to keep him behind *her* and in relative subordinate position. The Newfie happily accepts that he is low-man-on-the-totem-pole, and dutifully stays behind. (This is a perfect example of how males and females in a smaller group of dogs recognize a blended Power Ladder, as opposed to the separate "male" and "female" power ladders that help organize a larger group of dogs).

Look carefully at all of the photos. Only the Border Collie, the lead dog, is looking at the Frisbee. The other dogs are *looking at her!* They know the Frisbee belongs to *her* and her alone, since she is the top dog in the group, so their attention is on maintaining their respectful positions. *Their* duty is not to overtake their leader or overstep the limits of their position in the pack. The more I study these photos, the more fascinated I am by the culture of the canine. The happiness of the dogs and the peacefulness with which they play is impressive—as each plays his or her role while happily recognizing and honoring the roles of the others. *Beautiful!*

Below, I am using the same social rules and signals to communicate status to my dog. In the first picture, the dog assumes he is the one in charge because he's being allowed—unchallenged—in front. In the next picture, I am communicating that I am the one in charge, as I keep the dog behind me, ever so slightly.

THE DOG ASSUMES HE IS IN CHARGE BY TAKING THE LEAD POSITION. AS A RESULT, HE PULLS ON THE LEASH.

THE SAME DOG IS YIELDING THE LEAD TO ME, AND ACCEPTING THE SECOND-IN-LINE POSITION. NOW THERE IS NO PULLING!

When you walk your dog, pay attention to your *relative* body positions. Is your dog in front, or are you? When an Alpha dog wants to pull rank and make his authority clear to others, he *owns* the lead position! If all the dogs are racing to get the ball that was just thrown at the dog park, the most powerful and dominant dog is the one that gets there first. He makes sure of it.

The most significant, symbolic exercise that you can do with your dog is the Leadership Walk. (I show you how to train the Leadership Walk in the chapter "Train Your Dog...A Woman's Way.") Insist that your dog stay beside or behind you and do not allow him to creep out in front of you. This relative body positioning is so important that I mention it to ninety-nine percent of my clients who are experiencing behavioral issues with their dogs. Regardless of their issue, when the owner takes charge of the relationship in this way and starts acting like the leader his dog needs in canine terms, matters tend to improve. I'm even considering a new motto: *A Leadership Walk a day keeps the dog counselor away!*

4
You Don't Need Machismo to Train a Dog

Follow-through and Feedback (Not Intimidation) Controls a Canine

The Story of Piggy the Cow

One of my earliest child-hood memories growing up on our dairy farm was that of Piggy—one of my father's Jersey cows. Piggy was fat, hence the name. She was so calm, letting me pet her and brush her—even ride her! But most importantly, Piggy was the undisputed Queen of the Herd.

I spent countless hours around *and on* Piggy—what else do you do when you grow up on a ranch and have to pick your playmates from an assortment of farm animals? We were buds. At feeding time, the tractor would pull up to the feeding trough, and our ranch hand would throw the hay in for the entire herd. All the young heifers and other cows would come running, crowd around the hay and start eating.

Piggy would not run to the hay. She sauntered. Why rush? She was calm, cool and confident—almost presidential in a bovine way. As she drew near the hay, the other cows would scatter—making way for Queen Piggy. If they lingered a bit too long, Piggy would drop her head and neck, give a low, throaty "MOO," and the girls would obediently back off. If they didn't, she'd give a subtle but well-placed bump of her substantial shoulder and send one or two of them flying. Then Piggy ate her fill.

I did not realize until I was grown, the incredible lessons I learned from Piggy about power and influence! Piggy was, without question, the most powerful cow in our herd, but she achieved that rank and position *quietly*—without being loud or aggressive. She did not rattle her proverbial horns, get in anyone's face, or engage in daily fights with her pasture mates. She did not use physical brutality to intimidate. Instead, she used quiet confidence and clever control. And every time I think back to Piggy and her ways, I realize something new. Now I know why I could *ride* Piggy and not the others. Piggy was too *confident* to be skittish! She was, as they say in the South, "as cool as the otha' side o' the pilla." What a role model. I use her story today, as I teach dog owners the secrets of quiet power and control over their dogs, and she is always in my thoughts.

> *Being powerful is like being a lady. If you have*
> *to tell people you are, you aren't.*
> *—Margaret Thatcher*

Power Is Quiet and Confident

One of my all-time favorite TV shows of years past was *Happy Days*, highlighting life in the 1950s. A central character in the show was the leather-wearing, motorcycle-riding King of Cool, Arthur Fonzarelli, a.k.a. "The Fonz." The Fonz was pure confidence as he sauntered into a room, commanding instant attention with a mere "snap" of his fingers. He didn't need to yell; he knew the secret of quiet power.

Leadership—Five Keys to Power and Influence

Take a moment and list your own life heroes. Whom do you most admire? Who have been your mentors? Which figures have most influenced your life? Which bosses or professors or teachers taught you the most? The qualities in each of these people will probably be similar, and they are the qualities of true leaders:

1. They are concise, not wordy or chatty.
2. They are strong, steadfast and do not compromise their principles, holding themselves and others to the same standard.
3. They stay focused on their goals. They are not flighty or scattered.
4. They are unflappable—not prone to emotional displays of anger or frustration, however slight.
5. They are optimists.

This is a good starting list. What is *most* interesting about it, however, is that these same leadership qualities are the ones that play a role in *all* social animal groups as they sort out their leaders and followers. This is true for people, cows, horses...and *dogs!* Isn't that fascinating? The same qualities that I observed in Piggy the Cow, I saw in my mother and father. (I mean no disrespect, Mom or Dad.) I've seen them in many of my dogs through the years. I saw those qualities in Mrs. A, my high school English teacher, who taught me more about how to focus, meet deadlines, think deeply and work hard than any other person in my life. If we follow a faith, we will also see these qualities in the spiritual leaders that we worship or follow.

Control Is Power

Power is about control, not volume. It's what you do, not how loudly you say it. Rank between dogs is determined by *who can control whom,* not who kills whom. Power is determined by one dog's ability to *stop* or limit the behavior of another. In case you missed it, let me say that again: *Power is determined by one dog's ability to stop or limit the behavior of another.*

Though the sex to which I belong is considered weak, you will nevertheless find me a rock that bends to no wind.
—Queen Elizabeth I

Common behaviors that dogs use to test rank might include:

- Jumping.
- Guarding food, possessions, or territory.
- Mouthing or crowding.

Jumping

The dog that does not *allow* another to jump on him is demonstrating his power, and will earn a higher rank in the pack than the dog who tries but fails to stop others from jumping on him.

ONE DOG JUMPS ON ANOTHER IN A RANKING RITUAL.

THE DOG BEING JUMPED ON TURNS AND BARKS IN THE OTHER DOG'S FACE TO SAY, "I DON'T ALLOW THAT!"

Guarding Food, Possessions or Territory

The dog that does not allow others to take his food or toys (or come into "his" space) is also making a statement of power, and will rank higher in the social order than the dog who is unable to keep his food, toys or space from others' access.

Mouthing or Crowding

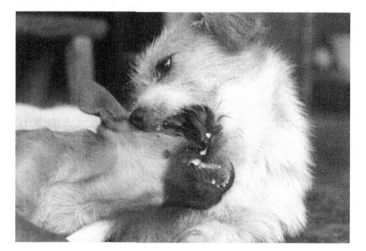

Dogs also experiment and test control or rank by putting their mouth over our hands or arms, or crowding into our personal space. These are subtle tests, often seen in puppies. They are asking, "Will you let me do this?" They are waiting for your answer. If you consistently allow it, the dog assumes you have no rank over him. If you *stop* him from doing so, however, you have scored a ranking point.

Does your dog jump on you even when you tell him not to? Growl when you approach his food bowl or try to take his toys away? Or does your dog simply ignore you when what you're asking doesn't suit him? If so, your dog probably sees himself as *more powerful than you*, and you more subordinate to him. Have *you* ever had to take orders from someone whom you did not respect? Now you know how your dog feels.

The Story of Margaret the Manager

The selection of a kennel manager in my boarding kennel illustrates this relationship between rank and obedience perfectly.

During our second year of operation, I decided to promote one of my kennel workers to the position of Kennel Manager. Margaret was the same age as the other workers (under twenty-one), and had worked in the kennel for the same amount of time as the other young people (less than two years), but I thought she showed great responsibility, attitude and other outstanding personal characteristics that I wanted to help her develop. I felt she was a natural for promotion. What I did not take into account, however, was how the other employees would (or would not) respect her new position of authority.

Margaret turned out to be fantastic as an organizer. She was great at scheduling kennel shifts. She kept the kennel in tip-top shape, everything was where it belonged and we were never out of supplies. Margaret had a very hard time, however, successfully supervising and controlling her employees. Instead of bowing to her wishes and directives, her staff would consistently fail to follow them. When she would call someone out for disciplinary purposes, often the employee would repeat the same offense the following week. Sick calls and requests for schedule changes were rampant. She had no real power, because she could not effectively control others' behaviors, and she had no control over others' behavior because she had no power. It was a vicious and frustrating circle for her, and for me.

In the midst of our frustration, I had a Light Bulb Moment. Thinking about it all, I realized that because Margaret was promoted from within a group of her peers with similar work experience, she was not perceived by her staff as having *more* experience, or *higher* qualifications. Because she was young, she had not the gravitas of age or maturity on her side. *She was not perceived or believed to be "superior."* Ah, hah! At last I understood what was going on. The staff was simply responding to their most basic animal instinct and the laws of nature— *follow superiors and ignore anyone else!* In the end, Margaret left to pursue other interests and I refilled her position with another manager with greater life experience. Almost immediately, sick days plummeted and performance rose.

So then, the secret to controlling your dog and getting him to do what you ask is really about *rank*— achieving power by establishing your *superiority*, and then using that power to *control*, without punishment, intimidation or bribery. A subordinate cannot lead, even with bribery, since he is weak. A bully that relies on threats and intimidation cannot lead, since he is an imposter. Dogs will follow and obey only a calm and proven superior. Humans are no different.

> *I will not be triumphed over.*
> —*Cleopatra*

Your Quiet Power Phrase: "I Don't Allow That"

Remember, it's simply your ability to "disallow" certain behaviors that gives you power over your dog. You'll teach your dog many commands and tricks with cookies and praise, and that's all great, but no amount of commands or cookies will actually make you a leader. Don't get me wrong. I'm a fan of commands and well-trained dogs, but without leadership, compliance will be optional. More on that in a later chapter.

The top dog in a pack doesn't use commands to establish his position. I keep thinking I'll walk into my kennel one day and see all dogs sitting at attention, and the top dog waiting to "release" them from their Stay commands. Maybe he'll pull out a leash to control the behavior of a wayward pooch. I'm still waiting though...Funny, the top dog in the group doesn't seem to need commands or equipment to establish his position of authority. The top dog's secret? *He knows how to disallow*. This ability to disallow determines everyone else's pack position down the ladder as well. For each dog, there will be multiple dogs above him that can disallow his behaviors, and multiple dogs below him that he can disallow. This is why, in dog-owning families, it is not confusing for the dog to be controlled by more than one family member. How convenient!

How Dogs Disallow

Let's take a look at how *dogs* disallow behaviors in other dogs. We will be taking our cues and learning our techniques from the dogs themselves. Luckily, dogs and their communication techniques aren't super complicated. They rely on just three core communication techniques—the 3 Bs:

- Bumping
- Barking
- Biting

Bumping

Remember my story about Piggy the Cow? She used the "bump" to her advantage in disallowing the other cows from eating the hay she wanted for herself. She demonstrated, without words or other tools, the fact that she was solid, weighty, substantial and strong. She had the power to disallow. Other social-group animals, including dogs, use bumping as a power tool. In fact, the phrase *"throwing your weight around"* comes directly from animals! We use that phrase ourselves, symbolically, to speak of our own demonstrations of power. Is it just me that finds that fascinating?

Barking

This one's obvious. We have all seen dogs bark when they object to something. Our dogs may bark at strangers walking onto our property to say, "I don't allow you here!" One dog will bark at another who tries to take his toys to say, "I don't allow you to have this. It's mine!" Or maybe another dog is crowding into your dog's space, and he needs to say, "Back off! I don't allow you in my space!"

Not all barks are to say, "I don't allow that," but they are easily distinguished from the barks that say, "I'm happy to see you," or "I'm bored and frustrated," or "Yippee! I'm going for a walk and I'm soooooo excited!" Trust me, you'll know the difference.

Biting

Dogs use their teeth to say many things. It's not usually a serious, I-want-to-kill-you statement, however. More often it's just "I don't allow that." When a dog is jumped on and he objects to it, he'll whip around and snap at the jumping dog. "I don't allow that!" he's saying. "Get the heck off of me!" If you've ever tried to trim the nails of a dog who objects heartily, he might have snapped at you. Obviously, he was trying to get you to stop; he was *disallowing* you to continue. Some dogs with an elevated sense of self and serious power issues might even snap at you if you approach their beds or food or even try to sit next to them on the sofa. By disallowing the behaviors of another (you), their power is being demonstrated and yours is being seized.

The Crucial Distinction: Training vs. Obedience

Training is about learning. Obedience is about rank and power.
—*Camilla Gray-Nelson*

In my opinion, no two words are more confused and incorrectly used within the context of dog training than *training* and *obedience*. They are used synonymously (e.g., training classes and obedience classes) but they are not the same thing. Training has to do with what is learned. Sit means put my bum on the ground. Obedience has to do with power and enforcement. *Who's going to make me put my bum on the ground?* Training is teaching the dog the meaning of a certain command or cue. Obedience is how the owner disallows any other response but the one desired.

Most dog classes are, by my definition, "training" classes—not obedience classes. People will call me or come for a consultation about one naughty canine behavior or another and tell me that their dogs have had "lots of obedience training" so they are hesitant to sign up for more. "Is he obedient?" I ask. Of course not—that's why they're here to see me! What they really mean is that they have been to a lot of *training* classes; they have not yet learned how to achieve true obedience. As I like to say: *most dogs are trained, but few are obedient!* Does that fit any dog *you* know?

Four Questions Away from Obedience

Did you ever watch the television show *Who Wants to Be a Millionaire?* The contestant had to answer ten questions correctly to win the million-dollar prize. In the contest between you and your dog to win true obedience, you are only four questions away from the "prize" of true obedience:

1. Who's asking, and do you outrank me?
2. Can you make me?
3. What if I don't?
4. What if I do?

Answering Question #1—Who's Asking?

Your dog must first ascertain whether he outranks you or you outrank him. Unless your answer is "I outrank you," the conversation is over. Rank, as I have explained, is achieved by limiting your dog's behaviors. "I don't allow that" is your power phrase.

Answering Question #2—Can You Make Me?

What you cannot enforce, do not command.
—Sophocles

Be sure you have a follow-through plan before asking your dog for any response. Exercise that plan if he ignores you. If you have no plan for enforcement, and your dog ignores you—*stop asking!* Every time you ask and fail to enforce, you sink to a lower rung on the power ladder. It is better not to ask at all than to ask and fail. This is especially true with the Come command. If your dog is not responding, just grab a cookie and go get him. Then, make him *glad* to see you!

Answering Question #3—What if I Don't?

It is important here to draw a clear distinction between "consequences" and "punishment." They are not, not, *not* the same! Dogs are strictly outcome driven. *They have no sense of right and wrong.* It is useless (and often dangerous) to use punishment in training your dog because it implies willful wrongdoing by an animal that does not know right from wrong in the first place. This is confusing and unsettling for a dog. Angry retribution on your part will be seen as confrontational instead of instructive. *You will not win a confrontational battle with a dog.* Personally, I will do anything in my power to avoid that sort of interchange. I value my health and safety much too much to do otherwise.

Distasteful or unpleasant *outcomes*, however, *are* understood by the dog if these are completely matter-of-fact and pragmatic. For example: hot sidewalks burn a dog's pads, so he will choose to walk on the cool grass instead. Table legs treated with a taste deterrent are bitter, so puppies choose not to chew on them. The hot sidewalk and bitter table leg were not "punishing"; they just represented less pleasurable behavior options. When compared to the alternatives of walking on the cool grass or leaving the table leg alone, the hot sidewalk and bitter table leg were behavior options worth avoiding.

> *Leadership is the art of getting someone else to do something*
> *you want done because he wants to do it.*
> —*Dwight D. Eisenhower*

In natural training, outcomes (produced or directed by *you*) are either pleasant or not so pleasant. You are demonstrating for the dog, "When you do A, this happens; when you do B, this happens. You choose, Grasshopper!" You do not punish for wrongdoing. Instead, you carefully weight the options so that your dog *chooses* the one you want. *He will always choose his most pleasant option.* Keep this in mind as you answer Question #4.

Answering Question #4—What if I Do?

Your answer to Question #4 will be most significant. Dogs are pleasure-seeking missiles! Just as dogs work to avoid anything unpleasant, they gravitate *toward* pleasure and pleasurable outcomes. (And I should clarify that this means pleasurable outcomes *for them*, not you.) How many times have you seen owners screaming at their dog to "Come!" with a less-than-pleasant tone and an angry scowl on their face? With every command, their tone becomes even more stern, then angry, then re-e-e-eally scary. The dog is thinking, "Are you crazy? I'm not going over *there*!" If the dog does finally respond, and the angry owner yells, slaps, or jerks the dog around, the dog is now thinking, "Wow. That was clearly *not* what he wanted me to do. I'll never make *that* mistake again!"

Your answer to Question #4—"What If I Do?"—must represent a pleasurable result or outcome for your dog! What's a pleasurable outcome? Here are the Top Four Pleasurable Outcomes on any dog's hit parade:

1. Touch
2. Praise
3. Food
4. Fun

Be sure that the ultimate outcome of your dog's obedience is one of these things!

Tone of Voice

Let not thy will roar, when thy power can but whisper.
—Dr. Thomas Fuller

Remember, your dog is gauging his response on what he *thinks* the outcome will be for him. If he predicts that the final outcome will be pleasurable, the odds of his obedience are greatly improved. This is why giving all commands in a *pleasant* tone of voice can produce better results than sounding harsh or threatening. When you give a harsh or angry command, the reasonable dog predicts that the *outcome may be unpleasant for him.* Dogs seek to avoid anything unpleasant. When you yell and your dog does not comply, he's not necessarily being defiant; he's just being reasonable…Hmmm. Sit on that one for a while.

Why Anger and Yelling Don't Work in Dog Training

Anger and frustration are interesting emotions. We get angry or frustrated when we are unhappy with a situation and feel powerless to change it or prevent it. We are out of options, out of ideas, our back is against the wall and we lose control. Well, well. There's that word again: *control.*

When we get frustrated with our dog and let that frustration or anger creep into our voice, we actually reveal our *weakness*, not our strength. When we yell in our attempt to gain power, we lose it instead. This is true in our human relationships as well, and in our business relationships, too.

To drive this point home, I want you to stop thinking about dog training and take a moment to reflect on some of your life experiences to this point. Think about the people who have been instrumental in your life, your role models, people you have most respected and most admired and leaders whom you most wanted to follow. Think, too, about the individuals throughout history who have changed the world, made a difference, and led or inspired multitudes. Take your time and put together your list. Do you have it? Now…how many on your list were yellers or blowhards? Funny. When I made my list, *nobody* on it fit that description! To the contrary, the people on my list—be they professors, mentors, ancient philosophers, spiritual leaders or political figures—all shared a few common traits. They were all focused, determined, purposeful, thoughtful, careful, fair and self-controlled. They were grounded, and solid and worthy of trust. They led and we followed. They were *leaders.*

When we yell, we are not leaders—either to our dog or our fellow human beings. Instead, we telegraph to the dog (or to our partners, our children, our co-workers or staff) that we are desperate, confused, or frustrated and have lost control of our emotional center. *In dog training, when we lose control our dog takes control.* Someone has to drive the bus, after all.

5
Pink and Proud

Embrace Your Special Skills to Channel Your Inner Leader

Lessons from My Mother

I love being a strong woman. I come from a long line of them. My mother was living proof that a woman can be strong, effective and influential, regardless of what she chooses to do with her Monday–Friday life. My mother never held a job outside our home. She was, however, one of the strongest and most influential women I have ever known. She didn't have a vast professional network. She didn't have a website, a Facebook page, or a Twitter account with lots of "followers." She was simply grounded, focused, managed her home and life on consistent principles, and spent her life reaching out to help others. As final confirmation of her immense impact on lives around her, the church was not only standing room only for her funeral, but the parking lot was full as well, with hundreds more of the people that she had influenced and helped through the years, listening to her service on loudspeakers.

In many ways, my mother taught me more than anyone about training dogs, even though she never trained one herself. She was not a yeller. In fact, I can't remember a time when my mother ever "lost it." But she was a stickler about the rules, nonetheless, and there was no swaying her. She insisted that we always speak kindly of others, that we be ever aware of their needs and feelings, and that we live according to a consistent set of principles. She made sure that she encouraged us children in all of our efforts and made us feel like we could do anything we set our minds to (and we tried some crazy stuff), but she didn't shy away from discipline, either. Most importantly, when she disciplined us, she always explained *why*. Discipline was not angry retribution to her; it was a teaching moment.

My mother knew how to control my dad, too. Now *that* was an art form! The dogs I train today remind me a lot of my dad: charismatic, charming and full of fun, but smart and strong-willed and used to getting their way. My father was handsome, successful and driven toward his goals. He was a tough customer. Mom knew what good dog trainers know, however: that you get nowhere with confrontation. Instead, patience and clever influence is the name of the game. Mom knew when to push and when to back off. When to give and when to take. How to use sweet influence instead of nagging to get what she wanted.

She would not embarrass my father by correcting or disagreeing with him in public. (I never correct a dog in front of his peers.) She saved that conversation for a more private time. In public, she complimented him regularly. (I am lavish with my praise when my dog has an audience.) On the many occasions I went clothes shopping with my mom, she would always make her selections based on "what Daddy would like." Given the choice between a shapeless but comfortable dress or one that showed off her fabulous figure, she would always take home the latter—"on approval," of course. "Your father would like me in this," she would say. I know what you might be thinking: that this was a downtrodden woman of the time, repressed and controlled, and sacrificing her needs for those of her husband. Oh, far from it! You didn't know my mom. This was a brilliant strategist and a great partner. She knew, in her own way, that if she gave my dad what he enjoyed in that small area, he would more happily yield to her wishes in other, more important negotiations. And I don't mean to suggest that there was a quid pro quo ulterior motive at play, either. She simply knew that in marriage, as in dog training, respecting your partner and being friends goes a long way toward getting what *you* want as well.

I remember one instance, back in the 1960s when the dairy business was good and my dad had a little money burning a hole in his pocket. He came home one day and announced he was investing in a start-up Japanese plastic company. Plastics? What does a farmer know about importing plastics? I noticed several closed-door discussions at home and more than a little chill in the air around that time. But my father was determined, and my mother decided that this was not the hill she wanted to die on. So he invested—and predictably, he lost. I didn't hear any "I-told-you-so's," but I found it interesting that the following year, my mother was happily drawing up plans for her new dream house. She was the designer in charge, and drew herself a state-of-the-art kitchen and a central vacuum, as well as other little indulgences. There was a pull-out booster step in the guest bath for future grandchildren and even a customized drawer for her silver—each spoon, fork and knife with its own nesting place, custom lined with tarnish cloth. The king had his folly, but the queen had her castle.

As a dog trainer, I understand my partner. I understand the power of influence vs. confrontation. I can win the important battles and not lose the friendship. Without being sexist, I believe there *are* various special skills that we as women can possess, and regardless of which ones are in our particular skill set, they can be our secret weapon in helping us control and influence others—including our dogs! Take a look at my list of "womanly skills" below. Don't feel dismayed if you can't put a check mark by every one; just capitalize on the skills you *do* have and work on the ones you don't. Not everyone can be Mother Teresa, after all.

- Persistence
- Praise and feedback
- Patience
- Empathy

Persistence

> *I've got a woman's ability to stick to a job and get on with it, when everyone else walks off and leaves it.*
> —*Margaret Thatcher*

Ask any married man who's been nagged by a wife. He'll tell you that women are really good at being persistent! Sometimes we get an idea in our head and we just won't let it go. We hang on to it like a dog with a bone, if you'll pardon the metaphor.

If we take this ability to be persistent and apply it to dog training, we are halfway there! Dogs are looking for a leader, and a leader is the dog (or person) that consistently gets his way. Not the one that fights the hardest or barks the loudest, but the one who ultimately wins the battle of wills. If you want your dog to Sit or Stay, don't give up until he does. How many times have I seen women ask their dogs for something, not get a response, and just give up? They find all sorts of excuses for giving up ("he's distracted, I don't know what I'm doing, maybe he didn't hear me..."), but the fact that they give up telegraphs to the dog that they were "just kidding" and are not a leader at all.

Instead, try being as persistent with your dog who doesn't Sit and Stay as you are with a husband that doesn't mow the lawn. It's simple. Don't get mad; just keep at it until you get what you want. Once your dog knows that you're not going away until he does what you ask, he'll start responding. It becomes easier to comply than to be bothered relentlessly.

Praise and Feedback as a Power Tool

When my husband does something nice for me, I try to make sure he knows how much I appreciate it. When he helps me with a difficult employee issue at my training facility, I thank him profusely and acknowledge his experience and wisdom in matters of employee relations. As a result, he feels appreciated and is there whenever I need him to help with that part my business, even though he works over forty hours a week at his own high-pressure job. On my side of the equation, I occasionally make time in my crazy-busy week to prepare a nice home-cooked meal for us. If my husband finishes every bite and tells me how delicious everything tastes, it makes me want to find the time and put in the effort more often.

Take advantage of your feminine talent for praise and feedback and use it on your dog! When your dog finally responds to you, *tell him he's brilliant*. Lavish him with praise and flattery. In my business of training dogs and owners, I find my women clients much better at giving praise than their male counterparts. Perhaps it is because, as women, we are generally more comfortable with flattery and expressing our excitement for others. For whatever reason, giving praise and flattery comes easily to us—so *milk it*! Like humans, dogs are results-oriented, and praise and flattery are results that they *enjoy*.

Patience

I am extraordinarily patient, provided I get my own way in the end.
—*Margaret Thatcher*

Patience is a life skill that women have drawn on for millennia, as they have lived with their men and raised their children. Some of us have developed this skill to a greater level than others, but we all have it in us. Just as the kindergarten teacher who maintains order in her classroom with her seemingly unending wellspring of patience, so we can maintain order with our dogs in our own classroom, called *home*.

If we draw on this innate feminine skill of patience when training our dogs, we are already miles ahead of others who might take a more direct approach but get distracted or have a shorter fuse. Training a dog becomes like the fable of the tortoise and the hare. The hare was quick out of the starting box but got distracted, while the tortoise took a slower, more methodical approach to ultimately win the race.

Nothing will undermine your leadership image faster than losing your patience. Be patient. Be strong.

✿✿✿

Nellie the Dog—A Study in Patience and Focus

My beautiful Dalmatian, Nellie, was a lot like my mother—patient, strong and clever. She was always happy and had an unusual serenity about her. She never tried to be "in charge" but amazingly she always ended up with what she wanted. Nellie avoided confrontation, choosing instead to use patience and cleverness to achieve her goals.

A typical evening in our home would go something like this. My husband and I would settle in for an evening of TV relaxation, with our three dogs sharing the family room with us—Arson, Maddie and Nellie. We'd give each dog a chew toy and start watching our favorite hour-long TV drama series. By the first commercial, we would notice that Nellie had her eye on Maddie's toy. She would not, however, make a move to take it away directly, as she knew that would spark confrontation. She patiently waited for the right opportunity.

By the second commercial, Maddie needed a water break. Before her backside was even out of the room, Nellie had drawn Maddie's toy to her own bed. By the third commercial, Arson would be asleep. Nellie's ability to move deftly and silently like a serpent allowed her to pick up his toy as well, adding it quietly to her personal treasure trove, with Arson never breaking his snore.

By the end of the episode there was Nellie, enjoying *all* of the toys while the other dogs were left wondering, *what happened?*

Empathy

This is where women can really shine as dog trainers. Whether it's innate or developed, we can be very good at empathizing with the feelings of others. Men empathize, too, but culturally they have been discouraged from spending too much time there.

Dogs have feelings. Being tuned into our dog's feelings can be a huge help in our training of them. Noticing when your dog is worried, overwhelmed or confused will help you know when to give him a break. Discerning whether he is defiant vs. confused, or stubborn vs. scared, will give you an invaluable edge in accurately and clearly communicating with him.

Stay tuned into your empathetic side. Dogs have feelings, too.

6
A Woman's Kryptonite™ – Stay Away From It!

*Fidgeting, Emotion, and Accommodation
Can Drain a Woman of Her Power*

A Woman's Kryptonite—Stay Away from It!

Do you remember the comic strip and TV hero Superman? He could soar like a bird, stop a charging locomotive, leap tall buildings in a single bound, and was the larger-than-life defender of truth, justice and the American Way. He was invincible. Unless…he was exposed to the mysterious element known only as "Kryptonite." Kryptonite rendered the superhero weak and helpless. Superman had his Kryptonite, and we Superwomen have ours.

I make a habit of studying powerful people. Those individuals who have the ability to move and influence others are fascinating to watch and listen to. Be they politicians, actors, corporate or spiritual leaders, they are not necessarily the brightest, the most knowledgeable, or even the most experienced in their fields. They have, however, mastered the art of making others *think* they are the brightest, most knowledgeable and most experienced.

In Chapter Four I described five traits commonly found in leaders and powerful people: being concise, not compromising principles, staying focused, remaining unflappable and being optimistic. There are plenty of books and self-help products on the market that assist people in developing these leadership skills. In this chapter, however, I'm taking a different approach: pointing out the traits that powerful people must *avoid*. All those fancy new power skills will do you no good at all if they are sabotaged by the insidious habits on this next list.

Powerful people consciously stay away from anything that portrays them as weak or uncertain or habits that undermine their powerful image. In making this list, I was struck by the fact that these power-sapping traits are often seen, disproportionately, in women! Oh, dear. No wonder many of us are not taken as seriously as we should be! I narrowed down my list of power-sapping behaviors to three general categories and refer to them as **A Woman's Kryptonite™**.

1. Fidgeting
2. Emotional extremes
3. Accommodation

Fidgeting

Powerful people don't fidget. Fidgeting takes different forms, from physical to verbal, but in all its variations, fidgeting says, "I'm uncomfortable and self-conscious right now."

A blur of blinks, taps, jiggles, pivots and shifts. . .
the body language of a man wishing urgently to be elsewhere.
—Edward R. Murrow

Physical Fidgeting

Physical fidgeting takes many forms, from playing with your hair to biting your fingernails to tapping your toe or your pencil, squirming in your seat, and so on and so forth. Watch Oprah Winfrey, Hillary Clinton, or old film clips of the former British Prime Minister Margaret Thatcher. You'll not find a hair-twirler among them! They sit or stand quietly, and their movements are deliberate. They may, in fact, be feeling nervous or stressed on the inside, but their outward demeanor does not reveal it. Their outward appearance is one of calm, cool confidence.

When women attempt to train their dogs, I find they often fidget physically. They will fuss with the leash, move their arm around like a helicopter, walk fast to keep up with the dog, and then slow down when he balks. They'll stoop to command, contort to be heard, reposition themselves in self-doubt, start over...Auugghhh! No wonder the dog can't figure out *what* they want!

Verbal Fidgeting

Much speech is one thing; well-timed speech is another.
—Sophocles

Even more women fall prey to the Kryptonite of verbal fidgeting. What do I mean by verbal fidgeting? I mean that many women seem uncomfortable with silence, and fill the void with nervous or useless chatter. Powerful people make a statement and let it sit there for maximum effect. They don't explain themselves, apologize, retract, revise or make useless conversation. They say what they mean and mean what they say. Nothing says uncertainty like verbal fidgeting.

❖ ❖ ❖

The Evangelist and the Power of Silence

If there is one professional that knows how to avoid verbal fidgeting, it is a professional evangelist. Whether their audiences are in football stadiums or easy chairs in front of television sets, evangelists have developed the art of verbal power and influence to the extreme. After all, they are persuading listeners to give over their very souls to God! If you want a lesson on communicating effectively and persuasively, watch a tape of the master evangelist, the Reverend Billy Graham.

Billy Graham was mesmerizing. He chose each word carefully and delivered it with conviction and passion. No "uhs," "ums," or nervous chatter there! He used words simply, clearly, and deliberately with no waste. His signature move (and my personal favorite) used the power of *silence*. After several sentences of passionate discourse but just before his most important point, he would go suddenly silent. He intentionally let his words sit there, bare and unabridged, as every ear in the stadium tuned in and soaked up the meaning of what had just been said. The audience was rapt and eager for his next word. You could hear a pin drop as the Reverend used the power of silence to gather everyone into the proverbial palm of his hand. And then he closed the deal. Your personal beliefs aside, you must admit that's impressive!

Whether convincing souls to come to Jesus or your dog to come in from the yard, you can learn a lot about effective, persuasive communication from Billy Graham and other successful public speakers. Don't chatter, beg or repeat yourself. Say what you mean, then close the deal.

Emotional Extremes

Frustration and Angry Outbursts

To wear your heart on your sleeve isn't a very good place.
You should wear it inside, where it functions best.
—*Margaret Thatcher*

Frustration and anger signal to others—be they canine or human—that you have lost control. This type of emotional extreme destroys your power base and puts you at a vulnerable, weakened position when it comes to negotiations of any sort. In dog training, you can forget about getting your dog to obey you when you yell. Animals, in particular, are acutely aware of the signals that convey relative power or weakness, because recognizing strength and weakness is so imperative for their survival. Even when you don't yell but your voice belies an inner frustration level, you telegraph that you have lost your confidence, your nerve and your power—and your dog will not obey you. Remember, obedience is about who has power, and clearly you don't have any if you're frustrated and let it show.

Smothering Love

At the other end of the emotional extreme spectrum is excessive, smothering love. This is not as common a problem for dog owners as frustration and anger, but it does bear mentioning.

Although every dog owner enjoys demonstrating their love, some take it to the extreme and smother their dog with excessive displays of affection, with continual holding, hugging, kissing, etc. When normal love and affection morph into this extreme form, the dog begins to see himself as superior to his fawning owner. Smothering love sends a message of subordination, *not* love. The successful kindergarten teachers—or parents for that matter—do not fawn over their children; they keep love and discipline in perfect balance. Smothering love is closely related to the next power-sapping element, accommodation.

Accommodation

In our human lives and roles as wives, girlfriends and mothers, many of us have come to equate accommodation with love. We clear the sofa for our husband when he needs to sit down; we change our schedule around so that we can attend our child's recital or softball tournament. It's what we do. All good people, to some degree, accommodate the people they love. It is a good and desirable thing.

In the animal world, however, accommodation is akin to subordination. When one dog "accommodates" another by giving up his ball, moving out of the way, or backing off when challenged, the message is, "You win. I defer to you."

In my own experience, this practice of accommodation has affected even my ability to direct and manage my staff. I'm by nature a very nice person, taught by my parents to be sensitive to the needs of others and to sometimes put their needs ahead of my own. In most of life's circles, that is a good rule to live by, but taken to its literal extreme you can become a doormat. Doormats can't manage or direct dogs, children or employees. Doormats don't often get all of what they want in life. In my own experience, I found that when I repeatedly accommodated my staff's requests (extra time off, changing the schedule to accommodate their personal lives, etc.), some started telling *me* when they would and would not work, refusing to show up when assigned, and generally developing a prima donna attitude. Apparently, my accommodations had emboldened them and sent the subliminal message that *they* could control and influence *me*, implying that they had more power in the relationship than actually existed. What a management lesson!

When your dog walks faster on leash, do you speed up to keep up instead of insisting that he walk at *your* pace? When he objects to being moved off the sofa, do you let him remain there, on his throne? When you ask him to Stay but he gets up anyway, do you let it pass? If you do any of these things, you are accommodating your dog, and cutting your personal power off at the knees. No wonder your dog doesn't take you seriously. Your willingness to accommodate is like saying, "Never mind." *You* don't take yourself seriously, so why should your dog? *Love your dog, set reasonable expectations, and then follow through without accommodation.*

Avoid all the elements of a Woman's Kryptonite, and you will be amazed at your increased effectiveness!

❖ ❖ ❖

TO BE LOVED, OR TO LEAD—What's Your Goal?

Many women come to me for help with their dogs. When we broach the inevitable subject of discipline, most women start to shy away. They want better control, but they don't want to discipline or enforce boundaries for their dogs as a means of getting that control. As I probe to find out why, I find a recurrent answer. "I'm afraid he won't like me," they say.

Have you ever known a woman whose only goal was to be loved by a man? When their sole goal is to be loved, women do stupid things. They come across as needy, clingy and weak. Decent men do not like needy, weak women, and *neither do dogs!* If being loved by your dog is your only goal, I'm here to say you may never achieve it.

The irony is that to be loved, you must first be strong. Only when you take control of your dog and his behavior will he truly love and respect you. Just as good men are attracted to women with principles, confidence and standards, so are dogs. *Nature loves strength; it abhors weakness.*

Instead of trying to get your dog to love you, try being a stronger leader. Stop accommodating his every whim. Set your boundaries and your rules. Enforce them quietly, but consistently. Give in where you must; take charge where you can. Don't be a doormat, be a Diva.

That's how you get a dog to love you!

❖ Part III ❖
Personality And The
Power Ladder

*Your Personality Affects Your
Position on the Power Ladder, and
the Same Goes for Your Dog.*

*Who Outranks Whom...and
Why Does It Matter?*

7
"Tellers" and "Askers"

Personality Differences in Dogs and Humans

"Tellers" and "Askers"—Personalities Are the Key to Compatibility

Just like humans, dogs have different personalities. All of Dogdom can be subdivided into those with "telling" personalities and those with "asking" personalities. Tellers are bold, determined and willing to take risks. Askers are more cautious, thoughtful, and thrive on the security of routine. Depending on your personality and that of your dog, convincing him that *you* are in charge will either be a stroll in the park or a climb up Mt. Everest. If you are a confident Teller with an Asker dog, he's waiting to hand you the reins and you are ready to take them. If on the other hand, you're a meek and mild Asker by nature with a bold and sassy Teller dog, your road to success will be more challenging.

Distinguishing Tellers from Askers: The Eyes and Ears Have It!

How can you tell if your dog, or one that you're considering, is a Teller or an Asker? Based on my observations and personal research, I've found that the best indicators of general personality in a dog are his *eyes* and his *ears*.

Recognizing a Telling Dog

Telling dogs know exactly what they want, and will *tell* you where and when they want it. They can be quite headstrong, and frequently challenge commands with a "Why should I?" or "Who's gonna make me?" attitude. For some owners, therein lies their charm. Just ask any devoted terrier lover! Telling dogs have eye and facial expressions that can be intense, focused, serious, determined, direct, staring, piercing, cool, confident, aloof, wild or sparkling. The adult Telling dog's ears are usually carried more up or forward, in terms of what is customary for that breed. Take a look at the pictures that follow. Notice a consistent theme in all of them. *These dogs just look confident.* They look sure of themselves and what they want. Often these dogs do not consistently seek human contact, beyond that which *gets them* something that they want from the human. Is *your* dog a Teller?

Cool and confident eyes. Base of ears up.

Look at this terrier. His eyes are cool and confident and do not reveal his inner feelings. The bases of his ears are up and forward. These are classic traits of a Teller.

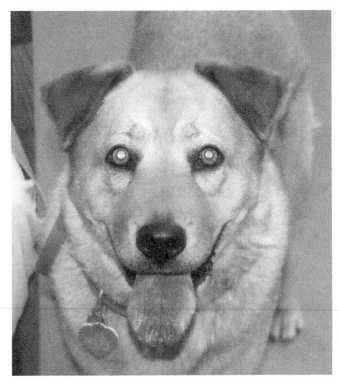

Direct eyes. Base of ears forward.

This Chow mix has very direct eyes, and the bases of his ears are also up and forward. With those physical traits, we can see at a glance that he is a Teller, not an Asker. So can other dogs.

PIERCING AND STARING
EYES. BASE OF EARS UP.

This dog has eyes that are almost piercing. And those ears are rigid at the base. He is clearly a Teller.

DETERMINED EYES. BASE
OF EARS FORWARD.

Can't you just see what this little Griffon is thinking? "Who's gonna make me? I double-dog dare ya!" His eyes have a determination to them, and the base of each ear is as forward as possible. A big Teller in a little package.

WILD AND ENERGETIC EYES. BASE OF EARS FORWARD.

Wha-hooo! This black lab is telling us with her wild eyes and forward ears that she is ready for action. She will *tell* you what she wants and expects!

SPARKLING EYES, FULL OF FUN AND EARS TO MATCH!

The German Shorthair is also a Teller of the energetic type: sparkling eyes, full of fun and ears to match. This dog will *tell* you when he wants to play and won't take "No" for an answer.

Identifying Telling Puppies—Under Twelve Weeks of Age

How can you tell if that adorable puppy you're considering will be a Telling dog as he grows up and matures? Look at his eyes, expression and general demeanor. Does he look confident, focused, determined? Is he bossy or wildly energetic? Is his tail held high or slightly above his top line? He's probably a Teller.

DIRECT EYE EXPRESSION. BASE OF EARS FORWARD (EVEN ON THIS VERY YOUNG PUPPY.)

Even in puppies we can see eye expression. In this Fox Terrier puppy, her eye expression is direct, and her *ears* are also beginning to take shape—*up and forward!*

DIRECT EYE EXPRESSION. GENERAL CONFIDENT DEMEANOR.

This puppy was the first to leap off the bench as soon as this photo was taken! Can you see how direct and focused her eyes are?

❖ ❖ ❖

Predicting Puppy Personalities—The Tip of the Iceberg

I often relate a puppy's personality to an iceberg. The tip of the iceberg—hints of a puppy's underlying personality—can be apparent as early as seven weeks of age. By twelve weeks of age the iceberg starts to rise and you can see confidence, exuberance, timidity and the full spectrum of canine personalities. You can notice marked differences in how each puppy looks at you, holds his ears and wags his tail. This iceberg of personality continues to rise and reveal itself until the dog reaches about three years of age. At that point, the entire personality is visible. Many dog owners are dismayed or shocked by "new" behaviors in their dogs as they mature between one and three years of age. In almost every case, however, there were telltale hints of what was to come in the puppy's first few months of age. What was there all along simply revealed itself over time.

No matter what you may have heard about the importance of socialization and early training in the development of puppies, neither will *create* a puppy's personality. Socialization and training can help a dog make the most of what nature gave him, but he was born with his personality—socialization did not create it. Timid or confident, puppies are what they are from the time they draw their first breath. Nurture (the way a dog is raised) can help a dog reach its full potential, but in my experience, it is Nature (what's in his DNA) that provides the raw materials and determines *what* that potential will be. In other words, a timid puppy will be a timid dog. *How* timid will depend on nurture and life experiences. A confident puppy will be a confident dog, as long as its life experiences are safe and positive. An active puppy will be an active dog. How active depends on nurture and training.

Recognizing Asking Dogs

"Asking" dogs like taking directions. This does not mean that if no clear direction is received from you, an Asking dog won't take charge of things himself. Somebody's got to drive the bus! But in his ideal world, the "Asking" dog is a passenger, and happily follows the course set by the driver—hopefully *you!*

Asking dogs have facial expressions and eyes that can be described as *soft.* Soft eyes can be relaxed, melty, squinty, gentle, woeful or uncertain. (Fearful eyes are not "soft," so they are not considered "asking" eyes.) The ears of Asking dogs usually hang softly from their head, or are held slightly down and back, rather than the "up" ear carriage so commonly seen in Telling dogs. They thrive on human attention and consistently seek it. The attention itself seems reward enough, unlike the Telling dogs that use human contact as a *means* to get something else for themselves.

SOFT AND GENTLE EYES.
BASE OF EARS DOWN.
EARS HANG SOFTLY.

This sweet-looking Beagle is an Asker. Just look at her soft eyes and how relaxed her ears are. You can almost hear her asking, "What can I do for you today?"

SOFT EYES. SOFTLY HANGING EARS.

Labs can very greatly in their person-alities. This Chocolate Lab lets us know he's an Asker with his soft eyes and softly hang-ing ears. (If his eyes were more intense and his ears held more up and forward...he'd be a Teller, instead.)

"MELTY", SQUINTY EYES. BASE OF EARS BACK.

This adorable Weimaraner just oozes love and subordination! The natural Asker signals are displayed to the extreme. Instead of wide, intense, or wild eyes, hers are almost closed. Instead of ears held up and for-ward, hers are folded almost to the back of her head. She's *asking*, "Just tell me what you want."

SOULFUL, SOFT EYES. BASE
OF EARS RELAXED.

What a sweet-looking Boxer puppy! His eyes are soulful instead of piercing, and soft instead of intense. His ears, even in their natural form, seem soft instead of rigid. He is an Asker.

WOEFUL EYES. BASE OF EARS
DOWN AND SLIGHTLY BACK.

This Dalmatian has soft eyes of the "woeful" type. Her ears are also folded softly back and down. [NOTE: There is a difference between ears that are held softly down and back and those of a fearful dog that are held rigidly back. A fearful dog will have *hard* eyes that are unblinking and glazed with that fear. A fearful dog is a *Teller*, not an Asker, and his eyes are *telling us* to stay away and leave him alone.]

COMFORTABLE EYES. SOFTLY HANGING EARS.

Another Asking Yellow Lab. It's so obvious when you know what to look for!

Identifying Asking Puppies—Under Twelve Weeks of Age

You're looking at a sea of puppy faces. How do you pick out the Askers? Ear cartilage may not be fully developed, so *every* puppy's ears may be down and floppy. Instead, look at the eyes and expression and the general behavior of the puppy. Does he amble instead of race? Are his eyes soulful, gentle, searching, loving or soft, while his littermates are focused, direct, confident, wide-eyed or wild? Is his tail held softly and lower than his back? He's probably an Asker.

This is the same Asking Dalmatian pictured in the preceding section. Notice those same "woeful eyes, even at nine weeks of age!

How to Determine if You Are a Teller or an Asker

You probably already have an idea about which personality type you are, but just to be sure, here's a little self-test to help you. It's roughly based on the personality profiling methodology used in the human resources field to maximize employee performance and satisfaction in the workplace. My profile tool can be used to best match people with their dogs. Because people and dogs are so similar in their personalities, it works!

Take a look at the charts that follow, and determine whether *you* are a Teller or an Asker.

TELLERS

The Controller
- This type of Teller doesn't hem or haw when there's a decision to be made; they are decisive.
- They like being in control and dislike being controlled by others.
- They want things to move along; inaction drives them up a wall.
- They don't want anyone telling them what to do; they like doing things their own way.
- They are cool, independent, and may have a deep-rooted competitive nature.
- They are self-starters with great self-discipline, working quickly and efficiently alone.
- They want to be admired by their peers, and are constantly trying to better themselves.
- They have good administrative skills.

The Passionate Persuader
- Passionate Persuaders can be the life of the party.
- They are more spontaneous and impulsive in actions and decisions.
- They tend to jump from one new activity to another.
- They love attention and are big talkers, tending to exaggerate and generalize.
- They are passionate about their dreams and ideas and easily draw others into their excitement, because they are naturally persuasive.
- They also seek admiration of their peers, but are more committed to group identification than are their Controlling counterparts.

Do either of these sound like you? If so, YOU'RE A TELLER.

ASKERS

The Careful
- Careful Askers are careful and precise (obviously!).
- They don't jump into anything, especially important decisions or actions.
- It is important to be accurate, so they take the time to research and collect as much data and information as possible.
- They ask specific questions and are excellent problem solvers.
- They like things to be organized and structured and tend to work slowly and methodically.
- They prefer intellectual, objective work and are more comfortable working alone than as part of a larger group.

The Easygoing
- Easygoing Askers take life in stride.
- They are not driven to set personal "goals."
- They don't rush to make decisions, and they don't hurry into action.
- Easygoing Askers would much rather enjoy life, surrounding themselves with close, personal friendships and avoiding interpersonal conflict.
- They are patient and kind, excellent listeners, and great supporters of others.
- They would give the proverbial "shirt off their back" to a friend, and others come to them for a "shoulder to cry on."

Do you identify more with one of these? If so, YOU'RE AN ASKER.

8
Love Match or Train Wreck?

*Dog and Owner Personalities Interact to Either Facilitate
Training and Control, or Make It More Difficult*

*Now that you know whether you are a Teller or an Asker,
you can better choose your canine partner...
or better understand the one you have.*

My "Compatibility Guide" for Dogs and Owners

Telling Owner—Telling Dog

Telling dogs do best with Telling owners. While the Passionate Persuader type of Teller does need to keep his or her emotions in check, all Telling owners are naturally confident and strong, and not afraid to make rules and enforce them consistently. Telling owners can persevere with Telling dogs because of their natural mental discipline and focus.

Telling Owner—Asking Dog

Asking dogs are often sensitive. The more assertive Telling owner can easily be overbearing with an Asking dog. When Telling owners are paired with Asking dogs, they must be careful not to be heavy-handed in their discipline (always a good caveat), as a sensitive Asking dog can easily be overwhelmed or frightened. The happiest dogs, after all, obey out of respect, not fear. A Telling owner with an Asking dog must be a leader, not an ogre!

Asking Owner—Asking Dog

Asking owners can truly find their soul mates in Asking dogs. Asking owners are not bossy like their Telling counterparts, but thankfully their Asking dogs aren't looking for Donald Trump to lead them; they just want someone a *little* smarter and stronger than themselves. While an Asking owner may have great difficulty enforcing their rules on a Telling dog, the Asking dog is not as likely to challenge and is more likely to say "OK, Boss," to his Asking owner. In nature, everything is relative.

Asking Owner—Telling Dog: Making *the Best of a "Bad Marriage"*

This is the relationship with two strikes against it from the get-go. It's like when you married that guy your parents hated. They were trying to warn you—from their logical perspective and life experience—that he was all wrong for you. You, on the other hand, were going on emotion, not logic. Love, as they say, really is blind. When the honeymoon was over, you realized your parents were right. Life with this guy was a constant struggle, and your personalities were in continual conflict. Some of you stuck it out, while others headed for the exit and "re-homed" your ill-matched spouses. I know I did.

When we have a dog whose personality conflicts with that of our own, it's also a struggle. Most commonly, I see problems when quiet, Asking owners have chosen active, Telling dogs. The dog, by nature, has more *innate power* than the owner so the owner has a more difficult time convincing the dog that he or she is the "boss." Without that basic relationship in place, owners will struggle continually with control. In some extreme cases, the Telling dog can actually become dangerous, defending his perceived status against all challengers, including his human family.

The solution? Instead of having a meltdown or confrontation with your difficult dog, patch the holes where you're losing power—like you do with your house before winter to prevent losing heat. Just as you can reduce the size of your electric bill by changing many small things about how you run your household, the war of control with your dog is usually won, not in a single great battle, but in a multitude of smaller ones waged subtly and effectively each and every day. Success lies in the margins.

You'll need to show your dog that you are consistently the one who makes the rules in your relationship.

- "More rules not less" will be your motto.
- "Because I said so" will be your philosophy.
- Your response to any undesired dog behavior will be "I just don't allow that, darling. Kiss-kiss, love-love. "
- When your dog tries to pull on the leash, insist that he walk at your side instead.
- When he tries to bolt through the door ahead of you, disallow it.
- When he ignores you, immediately follow through and model him into the correct response.
- If he acts up in the house, tether him for a while.
- If being allowed on your sofa or bed makes him territorial over it, don't allow him up there at all.
- And most importantly, if you can't follow through, *don't ask in the first place!*
- Pick your battles and win them all—quietly and calmly.

The message will be clear and undeniable to your dog: "I am qualified to be your leader, and you will enjoy following me."

Granted, a less-than-ideal dog match is more work than one that flows naturally. It's a daily job of staying on task, not backing down on your rules, and always being aware that your dog has his eye on your corner office, ready to take over if you blink. To keep your "job" as your dog's leader, you'll need to be on your game every day, but the rewards will be well worth it.

❖ Part IV ❖
Train Your Dog...A
Woman's Way

9
Learn to Speak "Dog"

*Body Language, Sound Cues and Feedback Techniques
to Communicate Your Power in Dog Language*

What Are They Saying? How Can We Say It, Too?

Dogs speak to each other in a language all their own. Learn to speak that language yourself and you will communicate more effectively with your dog!

Play with Me or Come Toward Me

Dogs request social interaction and play from their pack-mates by lowering their torsos and play bowing. The Dane in the picture is enticing the Doberman to come and play, perhaps wanting a friendly game of rollicking "keep away" with the Frisbee on the ground.

We can imitate this play bow ourselves, and get our dog to come closer to us as well! You'll see in the following photos that I am bending at the waist and lowering my torso *toward the dog* in each photo—sometimes bending forward and sometimes bending to the side, depending where I want the dog to approach me. As long as my energy and intent are happy and welcoming, the dog will interpret my posture as an invitation – not a looming threat. For this reason, a smile is always part of a play bow bend!

In each case, the dog will respond from wherever he is, and come toward me. This is not the result of training; it's just tapping into a dog's instinct to come toward the play bow body language signal and happy energy.

"I'm the Boss of You"

Posture

Few things communicate power more than posture. In a canine discussion of who has power and who out-ranks whom, body posture is loud and clear. The leader will stand tall, and the subordinate will yield. You'll notice in the following photo that the larger Anatolian is pos-turing by standing tall, and the smaller Bulldog, instead of challenging with his own tall and forward posture, is leaning away and lowering his posture in a clear mes-sage of subordination.

ONE DOG POSTURING TO ANOTHER TO COMMUNICATE POWER, AND THE OTHER DOG YIELDING.

When a woman tries to control her dog's behavior, the dog can't understand her words, but he *can* understand the message being communicated through her posture. Unfortunately, one often conflicts with the other. The woman will give a command but stoop lower to give it. Is she trying to help the dog hear? Trust me—the dog hears her fine. During training, she'll try to correct the dog with the leash, but bend down as she corrects. Her words are authoritative, but her posture is subordinate. No wonder the dog is confused! You are much more likely to get a response from your dog when you stand tall to give your commands. Not only will your dog hear your words without your bending over, but since they are coming from a what appears to be a confident leader, he will be more willing to respond.

Eye Contact

Effective communication involves at least two participants. I marvel at the number of people who don't look at their dogs when they walk them. How strange is that? I guess you don't need to look at your dog to know he's at the end of your leash, but there's no relationship if two partners never look at each other.

Eye contact is an interesting subject. Eye contact is very much related to power. Have you ever been in a room and felt someone staring at you? *Even though you were not looking at them*, you felt their gaze. You probably felt a bit intimidated, uncomfortable, and at a social disadvantage. They were in control of the situation, and all they were using was their eyes. Hmmm. You can use eye contact to help control your dog!

Dogs use eye contact to communicate power.

ONE DOG USING EYE CONTACT TO COMMUNICATE POWER TO ANOTHER.

When you want your dog to respond to your request, look squarely at him and give your command. *Don't wait for him to look at you*—he feels your gaze and hears you fine, even if he's not looking! Use the power of *your* eye contact to gain to advantage in the relationship—just as dogs do between themselves.

Taking Stuff

Taking things is a power statement. If you want to communicate that you are in charge, routinely take mundane things away from your dog—just because you can. This is a subtle yet effective way to demonstrate your authority and position. No fights required. [NOTE: Do not attempt to take items that your dog tries to possess or defend! Consult a professional trainer at once.]

This dog has a toy and I am asking him sweetly to give it up to me.

I am "trading" the toy for a treat. The result of giving up the toy is a *positive one* for the dog.

Once successful in taking the toy away, *I return the toy to the dog* to underscore that doing things my way will result in a *positive outcome* for him.

"Don't Do That"—"I Don't Allow It"

The power ladder in a social group of dogs is determined by each member's ability to effectively say, "Don't do that," to the other members of the group. Dogs use
- Growls
- Barks
- Nips

to say, "Don't do that," or "I don't allow it." We can use our humanized versions to say the same thing.

Don't-Do-That "Growls"

A growl is a warning. In Dogtalk, it means, "I don't like what you're doing; I suggest you stop, or I'll take more drastic measures." Although we can't growl like a dog, we *can* teach our dogs that a particular verbal sound precedes a more serious correction. I use "Eh, eh" or "Hey," but you could choose any word or sound.

Don't-Do-That "Barks"

A dog will bark to take his control to the next level. A bark says, "I really mean stop that right now. I don't allow it. " Again, we as humans can't make a sound that even comes close to a "bark," but we *can* produce a sudden, startling sound that gets the same result by using the dog trainer's friend—a training can. With just fifteen pennies in an aluminum can, we can produce a quick, sharp sound that the dog responds to like a bark. You can also use a quick shake of your keys, if that's all you have at the moment. This is especially helpful in controlling your dog's over-exuberant greetings when you come home from work!

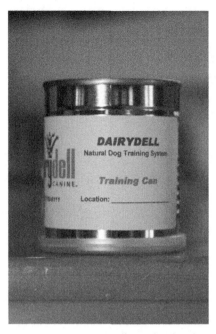

The Training Can: One of my favorite training tools is an aluminum can with pennies. A training can allows me to "bark" to disallow behaviors, but without anger or emotion of any kind.

The quick "ka-chunk" sound of a training can says to your dog, "Stop that. I don't allow it," and it can do so without emotion of any kind. Your training can *bark*, calmly delivered without emotion, can stop nearly every undesired behavior in your dog. Since timing is everything in responding to behaviors, training cans are most effective when located in more than one room. I make sure every owner whose dog graduates from my training school goes home with a full set of training cans! They are crucial to the owner's continued control and success because they help establish boundaries of behavior in real time. Even more importantly, the training cans allow a woman to establish her authority *calmly*, without ever raising her voice to her dog or resorting to confrontation. It's a beautiful thing.

Don't-Do-That "Nips and Bites"

When push comes to shove, dogs will use their ultimate control device—*their teeth*. But even then, most nips and bites are conversational, not confrontational. In other words, when one dog nips or bites another, it's rarely to fight. Most of the time those nips are simply a way to say, "Hey! I really mean stop that!" Since dogs don't have a spoken language, theirs is one of action. Even mother dogs will nip and bite their puppies to set boundaries and teach them Dogtalk at an early age. I witnessed these maternal lessons firsthand when I was breeding and showing dogs of my own. The puppies' mother would growl, pin and/or nip them whenever they got out of hand (out of paw?) Most often it was when they were trying to eat her food. She let them know straightaway that that was *not* allowed! Learning these important signals from their mother enabled the puppies to understand this language of dogs once they were out on their own.

Obviously, we are not going to drop to our knees and bite our dog's neck whenever he does something that we need to stop. We are able, however, to use a specialized collar that communicates this same "nip" message if and when it is ever necessary. Training collars can take many forms. All communicate boundaries to the dog, and some set these boundaries by imitating a mother dog's "nip."

A Review of Dog Training Collars—from Dog's Perspective

Head collars, harnesses, slip chains, martingales and "pokey" styles—so many training collars, so little information!

Generally, we will need a collar to train our dog, but how do we choose the *right* collar? In case you haven't noticed, trainer recommendations differ widely when it comes to training collars. One will advise a head halter, another will prefer a classic slip chain, while still another will recommend either a metal or plastic "pokey" style for your dog. The nerve-wracking part for the dog owner is that each trainer often *condemns* all other collars when they are recommending their favorite style. If a head collar is preferred, they warn against the evils of slip chains or pokey, nipping styles; if pokey styles are preferred, the trainer may "pooh-pooh" head collars as ineffective. What gives, and how can the dog owner make sense of it all?

A full, informative, and fair review of training collars is way overdue, I think. Let me give it a whirl from what I hope will be a broadminded, natural perspective—from the Mama Dog herself.

The purpose of any training collar is to *communicate boundaries to the dog*: where you want him to go, where you don't want him to go; what you want him to do or not do, etc. Training collars are tools to communicate these boundaries in Dogtalk. Each collar style will communicate boundaries in a different way, but all will mimic some method of control used by dogs themselves. It may be a constraint method employed by your dog's mother when he was a puppy or a more direct, adult version of canine control.

Head Collars and Harnesses

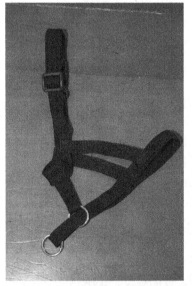

A HEAD COLLAR

You've seen dogs being walked in head collars. You may have even mistaken this type of collar for a muzzle. There are several different brands on the market (e.g., Halti®, Gentle Leader®), but they each have one design element in common: a nose band that physically restrains at the muzzle. When the dog pulls ahead on the leash, pressure is put on the dog's muzzle (by the noseband) to slowly bring his head to the side and interrupt the pulling. Harnesses also utilize physical restraint as their modus operandi, whether the leash attaches classically on top of the back, or in front of the chest.

From the dog's perspective, head collars and harnesses mimic the *mother dog*, who uses physical restraint to teach her young pups boundaries and to stop behaviors she does not approve of. Before her pups are weaned, she will often put her mouth over her young one's muzzle and restrain him this way until he stops whatever he is doing. (This is the rationale behind head collars.) Or, she will use her legs and paws or body to physically restrain the wayward. (Like a harness stops a dog's body.) As the pups mature, however, these maternal maneuvers become less effective—like trying to hold a child's hand to cross the street when they are twelve instead of two! Most will have none of it. Once a puppy has left the mother and entered life in the adult dog world, he is learning his boundaries from older dogs who use primarily the body bumps, barks and nips to which his mother also introduced him.

Most of us, however, get our dogs after they are weaned—sometimes long after. By this time it is not unusual for head collars and harnesses to be only marginally effective because our dog has already grown out of the developmental stage in which a head collar or harness would have been more clearly understood.

There is *an exception*, though! Certain dogs retain their puppy-like personalities even after they mature physically. The scientific term for this phenomenon is "neoteny." It means the retention of juvenile characteristics into adulthood. These neotenized dogs are consistently sweet, submissive, compliant and eager to have their "mommy" tell them what to do. Neotenized dogs can do *great* on head collars and in harnesses, because these speak to their juvenile characteristics. I have successfully trained a number of puppy-like adult dogs on head collars and harnesses.

Slip Collars and Martingales

A SLIP CHAIN COLLAR

Here we enter the swirling waters of disagreement between dog trainers. A slip chain (also called a *choke chain*) is a classic dog-training tool that has been around for years. Because, however, slip chains can be used in a variety of ways—from benign to dangerous—most trainers are respectful of them, and some eschew them altogether. I've never liked extremes or sweeping generalizations because I don't find them fair. That's the case for me and slip chains. Can they be dangerous if used too roughly on tiny dogs? Yes! That's why I rarely recommend them for toy breeds. Can they be dangerous to larger dogs when used too roughly or *in anger* by the owner or trainer? Of course. Are they inherently dangerous? Definitely not.

Properly used, a slip chain collar simply uses a combination of sound and physical sensation to communicate boundaries to your dog. A quick, but light snap of the leash makes a "zip" sound as the collar chain runs through the ring (like a "bark" in Dogtalk), and the quick tightening of the collar also sends a light "nip" message. The adult dog is naturally controlled by the *barks and nips* of his pack mates in Dogtalk every day. If your dog responds to a light "bark and nip" message from the slip chain collar, it might be a great choice for you. I'm using a light slip chain to train a Doberman right now, and it's perfect for him.

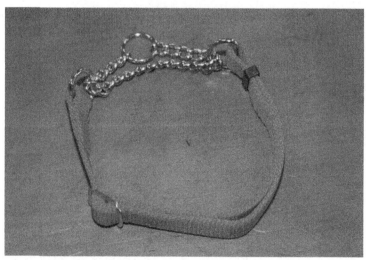

A MARTINGALE COLLAR

A martingale collar is kind of a cross between and normal flat collar and a slip chain collar. The part of the collar that goes around the front of the dog's neck is usually flat nylon webbing, with a tightening chain portion across the back of the dog's neck. When the leash is snapped, it makes only the "zip" (bark) sound. The "nip" is not there. Because there is no chain in contact with the dog's throat or trachea, a martingale collar does not have the same potential for dangerous misuse as its classic slip chain cousin. If your dog responds to a

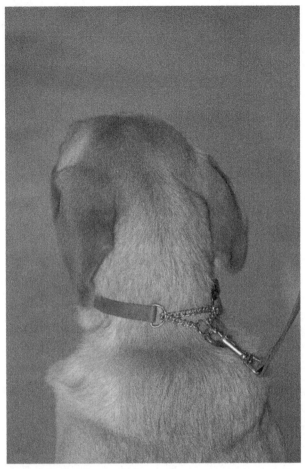

simple "bark" correction without a "nip," a martingale may work for you.

"Pokey" or Nipping Collars

METAL "POKEY" OR NIPPING COLLARS

Dare I speak of these? With the obvious exception of remote collars, there are no collars on the market more controversial than "pokey" or "nipping" styles. I'm talking about the collars also referred to as *prong collars* or *pinch collars*. Traditionally, these are made of metal, with "prongs" that apply quick, pinpoint pressure on the dog's neck when the leash is snapped. The metal versions continue to be the most widely used, but recently a more dialed-down, plastic version has made its way onto the market for more sensitive dogs. Whether plastic or metal, both collars work on the same principle—translating a leash snap into a "nip" at the dog's neck. This "nip" communicates a behavioral boundary to the dog in Dogtalk.

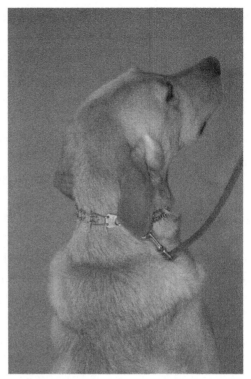

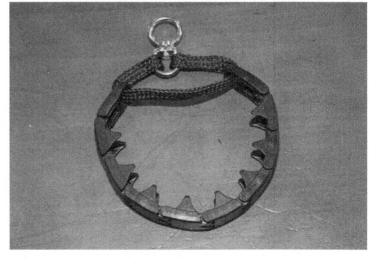

A PLASTIC "POKEY" OR NIPPING COLLAR

Can nipping collars be misused? Indeed! Are they evil, inhumane, or do they cause aggression in dogs? Not if they are used correctly. What is correct and what is incorrect? Now *that* is where the discussion

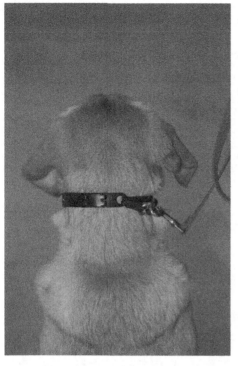

should be centered. When used quietly and without emotion, these collars can be a godsend for a dog owner; if used in anger or to punish, they can be disastrous. As with so much in life, the devil's in the details.

The sole purpose of a nipping-style collar is to communicate a "nip" in Dogtalk. It is imperative to understand, however, that when dogs nip each other, they do not necessarily do it in anger or want to fight. A nip between dogs is more often simply *communication*, as one dog defines a behavioral boundary for another. Once one dog's boundary is understood by the other, both dogs resume their play. No harm, no foul. Life is good.

When we use a nipping-style collar to "nip" in a matter-of-fact, non-emotional way, my experience is that this collar is not only safe but also capable of producing profound results *and* a happy dog. The dog understands exactly the boundary that is being communicated, whether it is to say, "Don't pull," or "Please don't move when I've asked you to Stay." On the other hand, I've seen these collars used to punish, to intimidate and to confront—and when misused in this way, they can indeed create a *defensive reaction* in the dog. In those cases, I don't blame the collar. I blame the "jerk" at the other end, *pun intended*.

Because pokey, nipping-style training collars can communicate so clearly, they are frequently useful at the beginning of a training program to quietly convey the leadership dynamic and basic boundaries. Once those are established, the trainer or dog owner is often able to transition down to a different style of training collar for maintenance purposes. This might take the form of a slip chain, a martingale or a head collar, depending on the dog.

Remote Collars

It's a shame that this last category of training collars has been so vilified. It is almost routine to hear them referred to as "shock collars," as if their very intent was to cause unspeakable pain and torture. Of course this is absurd, although the potential for misuse of an electronic, or remote collar is exponentially greater than for the misuse of other collar styles. The irony is that although the potential for misuse is high, the *educated and correct* use of this tool holds greater off-leash and distance training potential than all other collars combined. It's certainly a conundrum.

A remote collar allows an owner to give a subtle, yet clear, *I-still-control-you* signal to a dog that is off-leash, at a distance and otherwise unreachable and unmanageable. The signal is similar to that of a nip-like leash tug, only it is sent electronically. On one hand I have seen these collars abused by those who let anger infect their training, and on the other hand I have seen the world of off-leash freedom opened up to dogs properly trained on remote collars. Certainly, *any* use of a remote collar must include professional guidance! If you are considering a remote collar, make an appointment with a trained professional who is familiar with their use.

All training collars are communication devices. The *right* training collar is the one that communicates most effectively with *your* dog! It's really that simple.

10
Train Your Dog...a Woman's Way

A Guide to Teaching Commands and Changing Problem Behaviors with A Woman's Clarity, Consistency and Confidence

Before You Train

The following training suggestions are for the average, friendly-but-unruly dog. They may NOT be appropriate for aggressive dogs. Before attempting to train your dog with these suggestions, OR if your dog has ever growled at you or others, consult with a qualified behavior specialist to make sure your dog is a good candidate for leadership-style training. Most dogs take readily and happily to being led; others may resist. For your safety, a professional assessment can make sure your dog is of the former category— not the latter. If you need help finding a leadership-style trainer or consultant in your area, you may contact IACP (International Association of Canine Professionals) at www.canineprofessionals. com or iacpadmin@mindspring.com. Phone (407) 469-2008.

It is important to set the stage for your success. Too many people start a training program without taking the time to really decide *what they want from it.* That's like starting to build a house without a blueprint! It is imperative to understand that training is not so much about teaching Sit, Down and Stay, as it is about teaching your dog how you expect him to behave as a member of your family—especially when he's *not* on command.

Training your dog to be polite and obedient requires a couple of important prerequisites.

Decide What You Want!

(In other words, what you will and will not accept, behaviorally, from your dog.)

- Will your dog be allowed on the furniture or not?
- Is barking at the door OK?
- Will your dog be allowed to sleep in your or your children's bedrooms?
- How will you manage your dog's behavior when you leave the house or go to work?
- Will you crate train your dog?
- Will you need a dog run or a dog walker?
- Will the dog walker need to be a participant in your training?

Think things through, including your house rules and have everyone in the family on board and in agreement. *Then* start training your dog. Most people don't get what they want from their dog because they've never clarified *what they want.* How can your dog know what the rules are if *you* don't even know what they are?

> *The first step in getting the things you want out*
> *of life is this: Decide what you want.*
> —Ben Stein

Plan Your Follow-Through

Dogs aren't trained by magic. They may learn the meaning of a command by associating their response with a positive result (like a treat for sitting), but they will only be *obedient* if they believe you will *follow through and enforce* those commands regardless of circumstances, e.g., sitting when asked even when they don't want to, because you are prepared with follow through. Enforcement takes planning! Before you give a command, be sure you have a plan for follow-though.

A goal without a plan is just a wish.
—Antoine de-Saint Exupery, French writer

Teaching Basic Commands

Dogs learn through positive reinforcement. This is because a dog will only repeat a given behavior if he *enjoys* the result. (Like us!) After the command is learned, however, you can start insisting that your dog obey the command. This is where training is converted into obedience. The command must not merely be a suggestion; it must be mandatory.

"Let's Go"—The Leadership Walk

With rare exception, I include my Leadership Walk in every behavior consultation that I do—*regardless of the issue* brought by the client. Whether we find ourselves working on leash aggression problems or barking or resource guarding or improving the recall, the Leadership Walk is always part of the solution. *It is, in my experience, absolutely the most helpful command for transforming your relationship with your dog.* Because I find that most dog problems are the result of role confusion between owner and dog, the rules of the Leadership Walk are intended to clarify who leads and who follows in the relationship. The rules are taken straight out of the Alpha dog's playbook, the biggest of which is "Don't run or walk ahead of me because *I'm* the boss and the leader of the pack, not you."

To teach the Leadership Walk, walk slowly at first, with frequent stops, and enforce the following rules:

Stay in Your Office—the Executive Suite in Front Is Mine

Imagine that you are the boss and that your dog works for you. His "office" is the area on your left side, behind the "wall" that runs east to west across your toe tips. The area just *in front* of you and him is the executive suite. *Only you are allowed there.* Your dog is not allowed to leave his office on unauthorized breaks or to creep into your executive suite during your walks. *You* need to own that space, just as the Alpha dog owns it in nature!

1. Begin your walk at a slow pace with the command, "Let's Go."
2. The moment your dog tries to walk ahead of your toes, *stop* and correct your dog with a quick, sharp "pop" back on the leash. This is your nip-like "I-don't-allow-that" message. Reposition him gently behind your toes.
3. Begin walking slowly again, stopping and correcting each time your dog tries to move ahead of you. Do not be in a hurry.
4. When you can stop and your dog stops *automatically*, without a correction, you know you are getting the message across. *You* are becoming the leader of the pack!
5. Now, experiment with changes of pace: slow to fast to slow again. Is your dog paying attention and adjusting his speed in order to "stay in his office" beside you?
6. Success!

THIS DOG IS TAKING THE LEAD AND PULLING ON THE LEASH.

THE SAME DOG ACCEPTING "SECOND PLACE" POSITION. THE LEASH IS NOW SLACK AND WALKING IS A DREAM!

When your dog understands that when you say, "Let's Go" and start walking, that he must stay at your side, behind your toes and in his "office," gone are the issues with meeting and greeting friends or passing other dogs! There can be no jumping up or straining at the leash to go "visit" if your dog is obediently staying in his "office."

You may need a specialized collar of some sort to enforce this rule, but once you find the right one, your life with your dog will be changed dramatically for the better. Your walks will be a pleasure, with your dog walking calmly on a loose leash at your side. *You* decide when he can visit, when he can relieve himself, and when he can sniff the ground. As long as it's when *you* decide, your dog can still do all of those things, *but you are the one in control*. It is a game of Simon Says...and you are Simon. It's *magic*!

Don't Read the Newspaper on Company Time—No Sniffing!

During your Leadership Walks, your dog is not allowed to sniff the ground without your permission. Yes, I'm serious. I know it sounds over-the-top, but when you allow your dog to do whatever he wants, whenever he wants on your walks, who is leading whom? You are sending a message of accommodation and *accommodation = subordination* to your dog. Without exception, this will come back and bite you on the backside, so to speak, when you ask for obedience later on. Why should your dog obey a subordinate? He will see no reason to do so.

The dog below decided to take a break during our walk and sniff the items on the ground. He was reading the newspaper on company time! Once I clarified that sniffing was not allowed and required that he stay "on task" until *the boss* decided it was break time, the dog happily and obediently passed any distraction.

MY DOG HAS STOPPED TO SNIFF THE INTERESTING OBJECTS ON THE GROUND, IGNORING ME.

SAME DOG IGNORING THE OBJECTS ON THE GROUND, AND FOCUSING ON ME, THE LEADER.

Walk When I Walk, and Stop When I Stop

In a Leadership Walk at the Let's Go command, much of the learning is in the *stopping*. Require that your dog walk when you walk. If he hesitates, don't wait for him! Keep walking, and he'll just catch up. To do otherwise would be to accommodate...and send the message that he calls the shots. Dogs are analyzing every aspect of your relationship, especially during your walks.

When you stop, insist that you dog stop, too. Do not allow him to continue to walk until he runs out of leash or reaches the "office wall." When your legs stop, his legs should stop, too. *Out of respect for the queen, after all.*

🐾 🐾 🐾

HEADWATERS OF THE DOG TRAINING DEBATE:

The Myth of Aggression-Based Dominance

Unless you've been under a rock for the last twenty years, you know that the dog training world is deeply divided on training philosophy and methodology. I've been thinking a lot about this chasm over the past few years, and I believe *I have found the headwaters!* If I'm not mistaken the entire rift can be traced back to one, critical source: ***the myth of aggression-based dominance***.

When an assumption is made or an assertion stated that sounds logical, often no one bothers to check facts. If it's easy to believe, it is. And the longer that assumption is out there unchallenged, the deeper it is woven into the fabric of popular belief.

Such is the case with the myth that dominance in the animal world is achieved through aggression. The assumption that rank has been won through bloody battles, pain, and anguish—the Alpha male dominating brutally over his challengers—is at the root of the dog trainers' Great Divide.

One school of dog training thought is firmly rooted in the belief that dominance, subordination, and rank in general are established through this type of confrontation and aggression. Because confrontation and aggression with a dog can indeed produce negative, sometimes dangerous results, *all* forms of correction and the entire notion of outranking a dog are avoided. The trainers that ascribe to this philosophy keep themselves safely in the positive-reinforcement-only camp, opting to teach only new or alternative behaviors instead of correcting unwanted ones.

Trainers that do not believe that rank is achieved through aggression stand their ground in the "balanced training" camp, using positive reinforcement to teach new behaviors and using correction to stop most unwanted behaviors.

What a shame that so much divisiveness has stemmed from an erroneous assumption. And how confusing for the poor, unsuspecting dog owner that wades innocently into the swirling waters of dog training philosophy! One trainer says one thing, another something else; one book advocates one style and demonizes another. The next book says just the opposite. The poor dog owner! She's afraid to do *anything* and the dog suffers in the wake of her confusion.

Let's set the record straight. Dominance, subordination and rank in the world of social group mammals are *not* routinely determined through the use of force or aggression. All this to-do and argument over a myth! It's really a shame and our dogs, ultimately, are the losers. Read on.

Rank is determined one way and one way only: *the ability to stop another from doing something.* If you can do that, you have rank and status. You own resources. You get your own way. You tell everybody else what to do. I've watched this social scene play out for over fifty years, with cows, horses, dogs...even humans. Curiously, the ones that rise to the top of their social group—be they cow, horse, dog or human—are strong, quiet, focused individuals, not blustering bullies.

Let's take dogs in particular. Except in rare instances, when one dog stops another from doing something he doesn't like, he does it with *symbolic* gestures and actions that only hint at his greater physical power or ability, yet to be called upon. *Nature seeks harmony, not confrontation.* A dominant dog will stand on his tippy-toes to appear taller, in order to convince the subordinate to back off *instead of fighting.* He might body-bump into another dog to show that he is bigger and weighs more to hint that he would win a confrontation—*in order to avoid one.* He will bark and show his teeth, again to hint at his power, but to *avoid* escalation into a bite-fest. Even when a stronger dog nips a weaker one, it is conversational, not confrontational. The alpha of the two is saying, "I'm warning you to stop that. Don't make me use all of my teeth—see how big they are?" The subordinate dog agrees, gives up whatever he was doing, and harmony is restored.

In the dog world, correction is not angry, vindictive or confrontational. It is pragmatic. It is a means of stopping a behavior and achieving rank *without* fighting. In dog training, corrections given without anger can do the same. Dogs understand and accept correction; what they take offense to is *anger*. They are very different, and the key is understanding that difference

Sit

Teaching the Sit Command

There are several ways to successfully teach the Sit command. Here are my favorites.

Method 1: The Cookie Lure

With your dog on leash at your left side, let him smell a treat as you slowly raise it above his head and back toward his tail as you

say, "Sit." Usually, the dog will sit in order to keep smelling the treat. When he does, give him the treat. Repeat this until you can simply hold the treat, say "Sit," and the dog responds.

I INTEREST THE DOG IN THE COOKIE.

I RAISE THE COOKIE BACK OVER THE DOG'S HEAD, UNTIL HE SITS.

Method 2: The Tush-Push

If the Cookie Lure doesn't work, try this. Holding the dog's leash in your *right* hand, pull *up* steadily on the leash as you say, "Sit," and push *down* on the dog's bottom with your left hand. When the dog is sitting, give him a treat reward. Repeat as necessary, until just the word elicits a response.

I AM CAREFULLY PUSHING MY DOG'S TUSH
TO THE GROUND AS I SAY, "SIT."

ONCE MY DOG COMPLETES THE SIT, I
REWARD WITH PRAISE AND TOUCH.

Enforcing the Sit Command

When your dog is pretty good at sitting on command, begin requiring a response the first time you ask. Ask for the Sit *only once*, and if the dog just stands there, give a quick "tug" or "pop" up on his leash and ask again. The quick

tug is your version of mama dog's nip—you are saying, "Don't ignore me, sweetheart. I don't allow it." When your dog responds correctly, lots of praise! *Without enforcement, commands are just parlor tricks, and your true leadership is not communicated.*

Here I am giving the dog a quick leash correction for breaking her Sit command, by popping up on the leash. Then I praise her and softly stroke her to reward her compliance. I will repeat this process until the dog holds the command for me.

A QUICK "UP-SNAP" OF THE LEASH AS I REPEAT THE SIT
COMMAND TO THE DOG THAT DECIDED TO BREAK THE
COMMAND BEFORE I GAVE PERMISSION. THIS CLARIFIES
"OPTION B" (DOING IT HER WAY) AS LESS ATTRACTIVE.

REWARDING THE DOG AFTER A SUCCESSFUL CORRECTION CLARIFIES "OPTION A" (DOING IT MY WAY) AS *MORE* ATTRACTIVE.

The Release

When *you* are ready to end a command, bend over, clap your hands in front of your dog's nose and give a cheerful "Release!" command. Release means that the command is over, that the dog can move but that he is still working for you. It should not mean the five o'clock whistle has blown and that he can run off. As soon as the dog moves out of the command position, bring him back into the "office."

The Implied Stay

To really up your control and leader image, insist that your dog *hold* all of his commands until *you* say that they are over. Give the command, enforce it and praise it, but if the dog gets up before you give permission to move, *correct* him with a leash tug and *repeat* the command.

The Formal Stay

A formal Stay command is used to tell the dog that you are moving away from him, but that he should not follow you. It also means that until you *return to him*, he should not even *think* about moving. Never call your dog to Come from a Stay command! It will undermine the dog's ability to stay solidly and with distraction. (You can use the Wait command if you want to release from a distance.)

Teaching and Enforcing the Stay Command

1. Ask your dog to Stay with a word and an open palm hand signal.
2. Back up a step or two, standing tall and maintaining your hand signal, looking at your dog and holding the end of his leash.
3. If your dog moves, immediately but pragmatically side-snap the leash, give a soft verbal correction (Eh, eh!) and calmly bring the dog back to "the scene of the crime." Remember: your corrections must be quick and clear but without any trace of confrontation or aggression. This is not an argument; this is a teaching moment.

GIVING THE STAY COMMAND.

STAY COMMAND AT
LEASH LENGTH, READY
FOR QUICK CORRECTION
IF NECESSARY.

STAY AT GREATER
DISTANCE.
NOTICE MY TALL
AND CONFIDENT
BODY POSTURE
AND HOW
THE DOG IS SO
ENGAGED!

"I WALK THE DOG BACK TO "THE SCENE OF THE CRIME."

I GIVE A LEASH CORRECTION AS I REPEAT THE STAY COMMAND.

4. Repeat the Stay command *with a quick leash tug*. This underscores, in Dogtalk, that you really meant it, and do not *allow* his moving once he is put on a Stay command.
5. If the dog remains in a Stay for a couple of seconds this time, return to the dog and release him. Lots of praise!

You are teaching your dog that it is way more enjoyable for him to do what you ask the first time than to make you repeat yourself. Remember when your mom said, "I'm only going to say this once"? If she meant it, you learned to respond the first time you were asked because the alternative was not as fun. Whether you're a kid or a dog, it's all about results: option A vs. option B. All things being equal, we always choose the one that ends up being more fun for us and reject the other.

ADDING DISTRACTIONS TO THE STAY COMMAND.

You may then add distractions (like the tennis ball I have dropped), and reinforce that you still expect obedience, even when your dog has other ideas.

Down

Teaching the Down Command

If your dog is going to challenge you on any command, it will probably be the Down. After all, you are asking him to take the most subordinate of all positions—to bow down before you, so to speak. Some dogs do OK with training up to this point but draw the line at lying down. Some independent dogs cling desperately to their last shred of power and from their perspective, their dignity. The trick is to make the Down command a pleasant one, and not seem humiliating or embarrassing in any way. Here is where your self-control and ability to stay cool and calm will be put to the test. Remember: be cool, confident and lovingly persistent.

Method 1: The Cookie Lure

1. Choose a private and quiet area to start. Remember, this is a sensitive command for a proud dog. He may not want his friends to see him during this learning process. Respect his dignity.
2. Begin with your dog on your left side. Holding his leash with your left hand, close to his collar, let him sniff a tasty treat in your right hand and follow it with his nose as you lower the treat to the ground below.
3. *Do not give him the treat* until he lies down and his elbows are resting on the ground. You may need to start over many times and re-interest him in the treat. If you have a very food-motivated dog, this method should work very well for you. (If not, you'll use Method #2.)

GETTING THE DOG INTERESTED IN THE TREAT.

LOWERING THE TREAT, AND THE DOG.

Not quite there.

I give the treat *after* the dog's elbows are firmly on the floor.

4. Next, simply tap the ground with your finger, and when the dog lies down, give him a treat *after the fact*. Do this many times.

In the next phase, I tap the ground with my finger only—no treat in my hand.

After the dog completes the Down, I give the treat reward.

5. Finally, ask the dog for his Down without tapping or targeting the ground. If you reach an impasse, you can use the techniques in Method 2, below. *Do not get forceful or punitive!* If he responds to just your words, softly praise, give him a treat, and Release him.

6. Once released, spend a good deal of time telling him how smart and handsome he is! If he

has an ego, *use that ego to your advantage by compli-menting him and building him up when he's done what you've asked.* Come on, ladies, we can be really good at this!

Eventually, your dog will learn the verbal command and you will be able to give it from a standing position, enforcing it with just a small, lateral leash correction.

Method #2: Yielding to Pressure

For some dogs, no amount of cookie cajoling will get them to lie down. In these cases I find that gentle, continuous downward pressure on the collar and leash ultimately gets the dog to take the path of least resistance. His only choice to relieve the pressure is to lie down. *Be careful with this!* I'm not talking about cranking a dog to the ground in a show of force! That kind of pressure can injure the dog. It is not the force of the pressure that works here; it is the consistent nature of it. Even gentle pressure, if continuously applied, is effective.

THIS METHOD IS TAUGHT IN A FLAT COLLAR.

I HAVE LOOPED THE LEASH UNDER MY LEFT TOE, WHICH IS SLIGHTLY RAISED, BUT MY HEEL IS PLANTED.

I KEEP *GENTLE* DOWNWARD PRESSURE ON THE LEASH UNTIL THE DOG FINDS IT MORE COMFORTABLE TO LIE DOWN THAN TO RESIST.

1. Be sure your dog is wearing a flat leather or nylon collar (not a slip chain or any other type of training collar.) Attach the leash.

2. With your dog on your left side, let enough leash out so that it loops to the ground.

3. With your left toe, step onto the loop but leave your heel on the ground.

4. Slowly and steadily, lower your toe while you pull up on the leash. This creates a constant downward pressure on your dog's collar. (This is why we use a flat collar for this.)

If your dog struggles or flails, take your foot off the leash immediately. Start over calmly.

5. Eventually, the gentle but consistent downward pressure will cause the dog to yield. He will relieve the pressure himself by lying down.

SUCCESS! LOTS OF QUIET PRAISE.

6. Reward him with lots of quiet praise and petting. Let him relax, then repeat the exercise.

Be prepared to use your womanly patience to get what you want. I have waited up to ten minutes for a dog to yield—though it wasn't a Chihuahua, it *was* the proverbial Mexican Standoff. (Can I say that?) Anyway, the dog finally gave in. *I made him feel like a prince when he did*, and from then on, he couldn't wait to show everyone his Down command. It's all in how you spin it, girls.

Enforcing the Down Command

As with the other commands, like Sit and Stay, you will *enforce* the Down command by repeating the command with an "I-really-meant-that" leash tug.

1. First, return the dog that pops up from his Down command to exactly where you asked him to Down in the first place. The "scene of the crime," I call it.
2. Then repeat the Down command as you give a quick, firm *cross-tug* on the leash. Keep a smile on your face; no aggression here! No crabby, threatening tone. Just calm, matter-of-fact, option A vs. option B communication.
3. If the leash tug fails to get a result, revert to Method #2 and have the dog yield to the downward pressure on the leash, applied gently by your toe.

How you get your dog to lie down is not important. Being ultimately successful in getting him to do it *is*. Your power is in your follow-through, not your corrections. In a battle of wills, in the end it's not who yells the loudest; it's the one who ultimately comes out on top. *That needs to be you.*

Come...and Why Dogs Don't

Ah, the Come command. If there is one command that confounds and frustrates a dog owner more than any other, it is the Come command. There are many reasons a dog does not come when called—*all of them the owner's fault!* Let's review, shall we?

Calling When You Cannot Enforce

Remember the Four Questions asked by the dog before he offers his obedience?

1. Who's asking? (Do you outrank me?)
2. Can you make me?
3. What if I don't?
4. What if I do?

If you cannot answer *every one of those questions* to the dog's satisfaction, you are doomed to failure with the Come command, or any command for that matter.

Calling on a Hope and a Prayer

If you cannot answer Question #2—"Can You Make Me?"—you are doomed to failure. This is the main reason dogs don't come when they are called. Owners have absolutely no plan for follow-through. They are calling on a hope and a prayer that their dog will respond. When the dog ignores them, instead of taking action to follow through and make it happen, the owner starts *begging*. "Come, come, *come!*" Begging is ineffectual and pathetic. The dog ignores the begging owner, as he would an ineffectual subordinate. Begging is degrading. Don't do it—with your dog or anyone. Before you call your dog to come, remember my favorite admonition: *"A goal without a plan is just a wish."*

Calling in a Harsh Tone

> *Dogs don't know "should" from Shinola™.*
> —*Camilla Gray-Nelson*

A dog's behavior is not affected by what they "should" or "should not" do. He doesn't know "should" from Shinola™! For a dog, it's much more basic than that. His life is about seeking pleasant outcomes and working to avoid unpleasant ones. You cannot "guilt" a dog into responding, since dogs have no conscience or sense of right and wrong. Calling your dog in a harsh tone actually telegraphs to him that approaching you may well result in an unpleasant experience for him. You sound mad, after all! What dog in his right mind would willingly come to a person that is angry with him? I wouldn't do that if I were a dog!

Call your dog in a pleasant tone that says, "Come to me! I have the best party on the block going on!" When he gets to you, make sure he's glad he came and trusts that your promises are real.

"Punishing" the Dog that Takes His Time Responding

No one likes a "bait and switch." Don't promise a great homecoming and then punish your dog for not coming fast enough. He'll never trust you again, and I wouldn't blame him. How did you feel the last time you were promised something that wasn't delivered? Your dog's no different. Make him glad he responded, and he'll likely come faster in the future.

> *You don't lead by hitting people over the head—*
> *that's assault, not leadership.*
> *—Dwight D. Eisenhower*

Inadvertently Associating Come with the End of Fun

If you only call your dog to come when it's time to leave the dog park...the dog starts to associate the Come command with the *end* of his fun. If that's the case, you have unintentionally taught your dog *not* to come! How ironic. Instead, you must associate the Come command with fun itself!

Teaching a Solid Come Command

Two things have to happen in order to get a solid Come command:

1. Associating "Come" with fun and pleasant outcomes.
2. Teaching the dog that refusal is not an option.

Teach Come Like a Fire Drill

Remember fire drills when you were in grammar school? We loved them! They were fun because they weren't actually associated with fires or anything negative. Instead, they were a way to get out of a geography test! The fire bell would ring, and we would all eagerly get up from our desks, form our lines and march dutifully out onto the playground, where we would chat with our friends until the bell rang and we would all file back into the classroom. Fire drills were pleasant experiences, so we participated willingly. They were routine, so we knew what to do, and obediently cooperated.

Teaching your dog to come on command is like teaching children how to respond to a fire drill. Make it routine. Make it precise. Make it fun. Never associate it with anything negative. Repetition, repetition, repetition. Fun, fun, fun. Precise response to the command.

How to Teach the Come Command

The Come command consists of two elements: the dog *coming* to the owner when called and *sitting* quietly in front of the owner until released.

Here are the steps to teach a reliable Come command:

1. Have your dog on a leash or a long cord.
2. Assume your own play bow position by bending forward toward your dog and extending your arms.

Be in a happy frame of mind, so your dog does not misinterpret your body posture as looming or threatening. Have a treat in one hand. Call your dog to "Come" with a smiling, happy tone and start clapping your extended hands joyously.

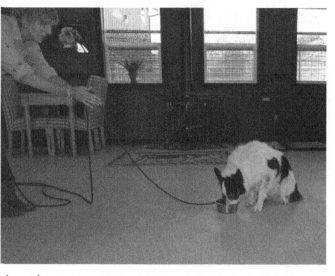

DOG IS DISTRACTED AND I AM READY WITH MY BACKUP PLAN.

3. If your dog refuses your first command, give your quick, I-really-meant-that tug on the leash or cord and call again – in an even *HAPPIER* tone. Don't get crabby! *No one wants to come to a shrew – even your dog.*

4. When your dog starts to come toward you, clap your hands vigorously to "target" the spot directly in front of you. Cheerlead him on. "Good Come! Good Come!"

I ASK FOR THE COME IN A HAPPY, EXCITED TONE AND ASSUME MY "COME-HERE-FOR-FUN" PLAY BOW POSITION.

5. When she gets to me, I *quickly* stand upright, bring my hands to my belly button, and say, "Sit!"

STANDING UP MEANS "STOP HERE."

6. Give your dog his treat reward, but do not touch him yet.

THE TREAT APPEARS *AFTER* THE DOG HAS COME.

7. Require that your dog remain in the Sit position until you Release him. Once he's released, you can pet and reward him. Make him feel like the Prodigal Son returned and make sure everyone around him knows that he has done something special. *Celebrate publicly*.

8. If he gets up before being released, you know what to do. Give your "I-really-meant-Sit" leash tug and quietly repeat the Come/Sit commands. Subtly teach him that you call all the shots in the relationship, but make your *rewards* for good behavior more obvious than your corrections. *Correct privately; praise publicly*. It's what smart women do.

9. Finally, release your dog and encourage him to go back to what he was doing when you called him. Say, "Go Play", in an emphatic way and let your dog run back to what he was originally doing and enjoying.

10. This way, Come is not the end of fun – it's part of it. Repeat this exercise at least six times each day, for no other purpose than to get a treat.

Calling to Come When You're Not Prepared for Follow-Through

What if you want your dog to come but you are not prepared for follow-through with the long cord? There are two ways to handle this: the emergency and the non-emergency.

Calling In a Non-Emergency

Calling your dog to come and *not* following through will erode your status and power. Is it worth it? Decide whether the situation warrants that risk. Sometimes it is smarter to *not* call your dog to come in those situations, and just take a walk to go get him.

1. Call your dog. But no more than twice.
2. If he ignores you, take that long walk toward your dog. *Do not be angry!* If you appear threatening, your dog will run from you. You want to *get* your dog, not chase him!
3. Approach him calmly, sweetly, with "kissy" sounds and softly clapping hands. If he starts to run away, *stand still.*
4. When he stops, walk a few steps closer. Do not hurry. Act like you have all the time in the world. Your outer confidence will convey an inner strength. Your inner strength will draw your dog to you.
5. When you get to your dog, *do not grab his collar!* Instead, scratch his throat with your fingertips, and work them up gradually to his collar. When you have his collar, sweetly guide him back to where you want him. You have just earned your dog's trust. From that point forward, it will be easier and easier to get him to come to you. You have not pulled a bait and switch or been disingenuous. You've been a strong, loving mother. You must always be the sweet, happy place!

Calling In an Emergency

Sometimes, we just have to call our dog, even though we are not in a good position to follow through. There are emergencies. That's why we teach the Come command, after all.

1. Call sweetly and *repeatedly.*
2. If you have practiced frequently, and earned your dog's trust, the odds of success are on your side.
3. When he finally comes, *REWARD* him with the most fabulous treat of his life. Every success is built on a previous one. The same is true for failures.

Heel

I don't spend a lot of time teaching dogs to heel. My basic Leadership Walk usually accomplishes what owners want most: a dog that walks politely beside them on a loose leash. To be technically correct, the Heel requires that a dog walk precisely in a certain spot, keeping the area between his shoulder and his ear lined up with your left leg. To simplify, I usually ask the dog to keep his right shoulder in line with my left calf.

Heel is actually a position, not a movement. That is to say that when we ask our dog to heel, we are telling him to come and sit on our left side, with his shoulder lined up with our left calf, and his body perfectly parallel to us. This, overly simplified, is "heel position." When our left leg moves forward, however, the dog must maintain his shoulder at our knee until we stop, whereupon he can resume the sitting heel position. This is why dogs sit when you stop while on the Heel command.

HEEL POSITION, DOG'S SHOULDER AT MY LEFT LEG

WHEN MOVING AT THE HEEL, DOG MUST *KEEP* HIS SHOULDER AT MY LEFT LEG.

Heel is a great command to use in order to reaffirm your *status* with your dog. Doing it correctly takes great concentration on the dog's part, so I like to keep Heel sessions short and sweet. Drilling on Heel too often or for too long can start to sour the dog on the command. It's not fun anymore. Heel becomes the canine equivalent of piano lessons. Need I say more?

Practical Household Commands

Stay Out

I love the Stay Out command. Even in a dog-friendly home, there are usually a couple of rooms that the owner may want to consider off limits to her dog. In my own case, my dogs are not allowed in our formal dining room or formal living room. Call me crazy, but I don't like seeing my dinner guests picking dog hairs out of the butter, or seeing them get up to leave my living room sofas with dog hair covering their backsides. It's just easier to keep my dogs out of those rooms. I use the Stay Out command for this.

1. I start with my dog in the same room with me. This is a dog-allowed room. I then walk into the no-dogs-allowed room, and define the boundary with a bold sweep of my hand as I cross the threshold and say "Stay Out." *I take my training can with me.*

I DRAW MY HAND ACROSS THE THRESHOLD AS I SAY, "STAY OUT."

2. If the dog ignores my command and starts to come forward across the threshold, I simply lob my training can in front of her. It "barks" when it lands at the threshold, and stops her progress. I take her quickly and happily back into the dog-allowed room and start over. I repeat this process at all of my "no dog" rooms or thresholds. (This is especially helpful in teaching dogs not to go upstairs without you.)

IF THE DOG TRIES TO CROSS THE THRESHOLD, I ENFORCE THE BOUNDARY BY SOFTLY LOBBING MY TRAINING CAN. (LOB, NEVER THROW!)

3. Very quickly, the dog learns that there are "trolls" at the threshold of all forbidden rooms that will "bark" at her if she tries to cross. (Like the trolls under the bridge in *Three Billy Goats Gruff*.)

STAY OUT SUCCESS!

Once your dog learns the meaning of Stay Out, you can enjoy your special rooms in peace and your wonderful dog will obediently and happily lie at the threshold, watching you. Everyone's happy and it's a beautiful thing.

Get Back

I use Get Back to define and own my personal space. When a dog crowds you, leans on you, begs at the table and so forth, he is not respecting your status. When you define and take ownership of your personal space, and disallow your dog entry into it, it changes the relationship for the better. By not allowing your dog in your personal space, you are sending a subtle but clear message that you outrank your dog and have more status in the family group. And it is your status, not your yelling, that will give you power and control over your dog.

To teach Get Back, I again use my training can of pennies.

1. I give the Get Back command and position my training can between the dog and me.
2. I then repeat the command as I move my can sharply back and forth, like Errol Flynn's fencing sword, to drive my dog *back* a few feet, out of my space. I praise her when she is backed up to where I want her.
3. I then defend my space by repeating this "touché" technique if the dog tries to move back in. Eventually,

you can ask without the can in your hand—just waiving your signal hand toward the dog. Easy!

THE DOG IS IN MY SPACE AND LEANING ON ME.

I DRIVE THE DOG OUT OF MY SPACE WITH MY TRAINING CAN AND THE GET BACK COMMAND.

I REINFORCE THE
GET BACK WITH
MY HAND SIGNAL.

Very quickly, the dog accepts that I own that space, and willingly stays back. *She who sets the boundaries is the one with the status. She who yells is the imposter.*

🐾 🐾 🐾

SUPER MOMS: The Job, the Kids, the Dog...Oh My!

You're home from work, trying to get some kind of dinner on the table, the kids are running wildly around the house and suddenly you hear, "Mom! The dog is jumping on me! He has my Barbie and he won't give her back!" Before you can wash the meatloaf off your hands to get in there, the crying begins. You're yelling at the dog, yelling at the kids, yelling at your husband for not stepping in—it's chaos.

I hear versions of this scenario every week at my Dairydell school. I explain to busy moms that the secret to getting their household under control and the dog better behaved with the family is *less yelling and better management*. What the dog needs is more supervision and less freedom.

Here is my advice to all busy moms:

1. When you cannot supervise the dog, don't leave it up to your husband or the kids. In the real world, it will be *your* responsibility. No worries. Crate the dog or let him hang out in his dog run. This goes for when you are at work, fixing dinner, or any other busy time that you are not able to keep an eye on the dog.

2. Young children must not play with the dog without you there to supervise. *Dogs will do whatever they want unless someone with status stops them.* They do not see children as having any status in the family, so they do not obey them. Instead, they ignore or dominate them by taking their things, jumping on them, etc. The kids can play with the dog when there is an adult supervising the interactions, ready to step in and take control when necessary.

3. Own your personal space. Don't let your dog lean on you, crowd you, or get too close to the kitchen table begging for food, etc. Define your personal space and then *own* it. This is a sign of status. If your dog gets too close, use a series of quick shakes of a penny-filled training can* or your keys between you and him to "drive" him back a bit. Owning and protecting your personal space tells your dog that you have a higher status than he, and will make you more effective in getting him to listen to you later on.**

4. Don't allow your dog to jump on you. Teach him the "Off" command, using your training can as a "bark." When he tries to jump on you, give a quick, *calm*, but decisive shake of the can directly in front of his eyes.** (This is where dogs bark at each other to say, "Don't jump on me—I outrank you.") Don't lurch—you will look confrontational. Don't push the dog off you—dogs love to be touched.

5. If your dog jumps on visitors when they arrive, have a tether and a dog bed ready by the front door. This tether can be a leash or a chew-proof tie down, secured to something sturdy or an eyebolt in the baseboard. When the doorbell rings, quickly attach the dog to his tether near his bed, and softly say "Manners", as you open the door. The tether will keep him where he is and prevent

him from jumping all over the visitors. When the dog is sufficiently calm, you can attach a leash to his collar and un-tether him. The leash will allow you to stay in control of the situation, calmly teaching him that jumping and bumping guests is simply never allowed in your household.

6. For dogs that continually misbehave in the house, even when you are supervising, try having them drag a leash whenever they are indoors. This will give you quicker control when needed. Remember, when you cannot supervise the dog, *put him away* in his crate or dog run.

These are just a few tips to help you calm the chaos and regain control of your dog and your household. Oh yes—here's one more tip: *Sign up for dog training!*

*You can make your own training can by putting fifteen pennies into an empty soda can and duct taping over the hole. Professional training cans may also be purchased in sets with full instructions at my **www. dogtalkstore.com**.

**If your dog has a history of growling at you or others, DO NOT use a penny can correction without consulting FIRST with a professional trainer.

Go to Your Spot/Stay in Your Spot

This is my favorite and most-used household command! Anyone who loves living with dogs has got to admit there are some situations when you just need your dog out from underfoot, no matter how much you love him. Go to Your Spot allows your dog to be near the action, but not part of it. It is a way to confine your dog without putting him in a crate or taking him out of the room. It is the perfect command for family dinnertime, homework time, when friends come to visit or anytime you need your dog to chill and stay put while events go on around him.

Teaching Go to Your Spot:

1. Start with your dog on his leash and training collar.
2. Have several "spots" ready to practice on: a dog bed, a rug, a blanket—anything with a defined edge that will represent a physical boundary to the dog. You want this to be a generalized command, useful anywhere you happen to be at the time.
3. Say, "Go to Your Spot", as you lead the dog onto the spot you are pointing to.

DIRECTING THE DOG TO THE SPOT.

4. When he has all four feet on the spot, give your dog a treat reward and say, "Stay in Your Spot", with a sweeping hand gesture.

TELLING THE DOG TO STAY IN HIS SPOT.

5. Drop the leash and walk away.
6. If the dog walks off the spot, take him "back to the scene of the crime" and repeat the command, "Stay in Your Spot," with a quick, I-really-meant-that tug on the leash.

My dog has crawled off of her spot...

...so I take her back to "the scene of the crime,"

AND GIVE A LEASH CORRECTION
AS I REPEAT THE COMMAND,
"STAY IN YOUR SPOT."

7. Walk away again. The dog should begin to understand that it is much more fun for him to stay in his spot when asked, than to repeatedly get up and leave. If he gets up again, the leash tug should be quicker and more convincing. NEVER BE ANGRY, however. It's just option A vs. option B to the dog, and it is your responsibility to make the options clearly different. When your way seems clearly better to the dog than his way – SUCCESS!

STAY IN YOUR SPOT SUCCESS!

8. Once your dog is getting the concept of Stay in Your Spot, introduce distractions, like the doorbell or tennis balls or the kids running around the room. Insist that he remain on his Spot, regardless of the distractions.

9. When he is successful, make him feel accomplished and special. Tell him he's smart and handsome (or beautiful as the case may be). Give him a treat. Do whatever helps your dog understand that staying in his Spot is the best thing ever, and certainly better than not staying there.

10. To release your dog from his Spot, be sure to go back to your dog before releasing him. Give an enthusiastic "Release!" command, with two claps of your hands directly in front of his nose. Coming back to your dog before releasing him from his spot will help keep your dog solidly on his spot, and not anticipating any release from a distance.

"RELEASE!" FROM THE COMMAND.

If you teach this command and use it, you will no doubt find it to be one of your favorites, as it is mine. You will thank me every day for it!

Teaching Boundaries

Does your dog fly out the door when it is opened? Run into the street from the front lawn? Leave the room you are in to maraud around the house on his own? Your dog could use some boundary training!

To teach your dog safe and practical boundaries, you need just three things:

1. A dog.
2. A long line.
3. A regular or training collar.

With a long line attached to your dog via his collar, you can teach him to respect virtually any boundary— whether it is the edge of the front lawn, the threshold of your garage or front door, or the doorway of the room you are in. Here's how:

1. Choose the boundary you want to teach.
2. Put a collar on your dog (either a flat collar or a training collar like a slip chain, a martingale or pokey style.)
3. Attach a long line of fifteen to thirty feet to the collar and hold the other end.
4. When you dog reaches the boundary you want to teach, "pop" the long line to give a quick, sharp, "that's far enough" message. If your dog tries again to cross the boundary, "pop" the line again. The long line and collar are, in essence, acting like an invisible fence, which the dog encounters each time he tries to cross the boundary.

Repeat this several times. Enlist the help of a friend or family member as an assistant, and have them cross the boundary as you reinforce the do-not-pass rule for your dog. Very soon, you will have a dog that will *not* bolt through the door, run across the street or leave the room that you are in, because he will believe and respect the boundaries that you have set for him.

Try it! This is especially effective for young puppies, but can work with any age dog. Here's to a safer life ahead through better boundaries for our dogs!

Leave It

Leave It is a command that tells your dog to turn his attention *away* from something he's considering. It might be a lump of unknown origin on the sidewalk that you do not want him to eat, the pill you accidentally dropped on the bathroom floor or the bright green puddle of deadly antifreeze in the parking lot. Leave It can be a life-saving command!

To teach Leave It, what you really want to communicate to your dog is that *you do not allow* him to touch that which he's considering eating, licking, grabbing, etc. You are setting another behavioral boundary. If he insists on grabbing, licking or eating the forbidden fruit, there will be a consequence of sorts. On the other hand, if he compliantly turns away from his temptation, this will result in something pleasant (petting, praising and/or a treat.) You have again set up option A vs. option B.

To teach Leave It:

1. First, teach your dog that "Leave It" means that something better is coming his way. Say, "Leave It," and immediately give your dog a treat. Repeat this many times, until your dog begins to look for his treat whenever you say, "Leave It." In saying "Leave It," and then giving my dog a treat, I am creating a *conditioned response*. Remember Pavlov?

WORD ASSOCIATION: "LEAVE IT" MEANS "SOMETHING BETTER IS COMING."

2. Put a dog treat or some other temptation on the floor. (I used tennis balls in the photos that follow.)
3. With a training can in one hand, lead your dog, on leash, to the temptation.
4. Now, teach your dog that he needs to *resist temptation* in order to get the Leave It reward. When you reach the temptation, say, "Leave It." If your dog makes a move toward the temptation, quickly *drop the training* can on the temptation before he gets it. You have just made the temptation "bark" at him as a result of not "leaving it" and resisting!

ENFORCING LEAVE IT BY DROPPING THE TRAINING CAN ON THE FORBIDDEN ITEM.

5. When your dog jumps back, praise and reward him with the treat from your hand. *Do not let him have the temptation that is on the floor.* Pick it up and put it away.

REWARDING THE DOG FOR A SUCCESSFUL LEAVE IT WITH TENNIS BALL DISTRACTIONS.

6. When you say "Leave It," your dog should immediately turn away from temptation. It could save his life someday. In the photo below, my dog is able to resist a boatload of temptations—two tennis balls, her favorite Kong toy *and* a bowl of food!

LEAVE IT SUCCESS!

Manners

Closely related to Leave It is my command, "Manners." In essence, it's a Leave It for people. When greeting guests and friends, I use Manners instead of Leave It to prevent jumping and humping. Although you want to teach your dog to resist the temptation to jump on guests, using "Leave It" can make your friends feel like that piece of rotten meat on the sidewalk. Not very welcoming.

Teach Manners *on leash*:

1. I start by letting a friend approach my dog on leash, with the dog at my side and the leash slack.
2. As they approach, I say, "Manners," quietly to my dog.
3. If my dog starts to move forward toward the person, I ask them to stop. I quickly give a snap *back* on the training collar, get my dog back into her "office" beside me, and softly repeat the Manners command. My friend stands still until the dog willingly settles into her position at my side and I give the signal to again approach.
4. When my friend is able to pet the dog without the dog rushing forward to jump, I praise the dog.

When guests arrive at your home, quickly attach a leash to your dog's collar and use the Manners command to enforce civilized and polite greetings.

Common Behavior Problems

Barking

I think dogs should bark to alert us of approaching danger. I also think they should stop barking when we ask them to.

Once again, getting a dog to stop barking when asked is about making barking *less pleasant* after you've asked for it to stop. There are a number of ways to do this, depending on the dog's determination to bark.

[NOTE: If you have an excessively shy or timid dog, do not invite people to pet him. It's too stressful for him! My "SHY DOG" alert vest, worn by the dog, can be very helpful in maintaining his comfort zone. See "Essential Tools for Dog Training Success" for ordering information.]

If your dog is barking:

1. Ask him to "Hush."
2. If he continues to bark, spray the dog with a trigger spray bottle of water or water with an added deterrent. (Some people use lemon juice, others vinegar; I use my "Don't Do That!" spray, a dilute mixture of citronella and water.)

CORRECTING A BARKING DOG WITH A SPRAY BOTTLE.

MY ORIGINAL "DON'T DO THAT!" SPRAY

3. Praise him softly when he stops barking.

If your dog is still determined to bark:

1. Try a shake of your training can to enforce your Hush command. A sudden, quick shake of a can filled with pennies mimics an Alpha dog's bark of disapproval—you are *disallowing* your dog to continue barking. *Do not sound mad or angry at your dog!* That would make things worse.
2. Praise him softly when he stops barking.

If the training can is not effective, you must find another consequence (result) that the dog considers worth avoiding. A citronella spray collar may do the trick, since the burst of citronella mist that occurs with each bark is distasteful to most dogs. If the citronella collar does not work, consult a dog training professional that is familiar with other forms of bark control.

A TYPICAL CITRONELLA SPRAY COLLAR

Jumping

Ah, jumping. Such a universal problem for dog owners, yet so *easy* to fix!

If you want your dog to stop jumping on you, do what dogs do. The dog that objects to being jumped on simply *barks* at the jumper, to say, "I don't allow that."

1. Hold your training can in one hand, low at your side.
2. When your dog jumps up, say "Off," and *meet his leap* with a quick and sudden *shake of the can directly in front of his eyes.* Do not yell or sound mad. Be matter-of-fact. Do not bend or push your dog off you. To do so would be to look uncertain and reward your dog with the gift of touch.

This young puppy likes to jump on people.

I make jumping less pleasurable by "barking" with my training can.

VOILA! NO JUMPING!

3. When your dog resists the urge to jump up and remains with four-on-the-floor, *softly praise him*. Withhold your touch until you see that he has given up the idea of jumping. If you touch too soon, you will be rewarding and encouraging his desire to jump, and he will do so again.

Digging

Dogs that are not supervised will do what nature has programmed them to do. Digging is one of those things. It is a natural behavior for a dog and a fun activity for a bored dog. A bored, unsupervised dog will do whatever is fun.

If you do not want your dog to dig in your yard, the solution is as simple as 1-2-3:

1. Supervise him or put him away!
2. Disallow digging if you see him start (using the spray of a hose, a lob of your training can, etc.).
3. Put your dog in a crate or dog run when you leave.

It's as simple as that.

❖ ❖ ❖

#1 Cause of Dog Behavior Issues: TOO MUCH FREEDOM!

When dealing with dogs, it's not what we do that matters but how the dog *perceives* what we do. When we give our dog too much freedom—the freedom to patrol the entire yard or property while we are gone, the freedom to hike off leash, the freedom to roam about the house and explore with no restrictions, the freedom to sniff, pull, and investigate at will on our walks...we are sending a potentially dangerous message.

In a dog's world, freedom is related to power. What you are allowed or not allowed to do is directly related to your position in the pack hierarchy. The dog at the bottom of the social hierarchy has relatively little freedom. He cannot possess anything, as all resources are controlled and possessed by the top dog. He cannot eat when he feels like it, as the more dominant dogs eat their fill first, leaving him the leftovers. He can't even take a mate, as breeding rights are the exclusive property of the top dog. He follows direction, is obedient to others...but *happily* accepts his place in the group.

The top dog, on the other hand, has unlimited freedom. When you are at the top, there is no one above you to say, "I don't allow that." If no one is controlling a dog's behavior then he is, by definition, the One in Charge. *His freedom is evidence of his rank.* As top dog, everything belongs to him and nothing is denied him. He is free to go where he wants, do what he wants and have what he wants. Does *your* dog go where he wants, do what he wants and have what he wants? Think about it. We may think we're expressing love by granting our dog such leeway, but we could, instead, be creating a monster.

When we give our dog unrestricted freedom, *from his perspective we are telling him that he is in charge* and that he need not listen to anyone. Since he *makes* the rules, he need not follow them. When we ask that dog to do something for us, or stop doing something else, we will be ignored or worse—disciplined with a bite, as in, "How dare you tell the boss what to do!" Have you ever been ignored by your dog? Has your dog ever growled at you? Now you know why.

Control your dog. Limit his freedoms. Even if there is no practical reason to do so, do it anyway—*because you can*. For a happy, safe relationship with a dog, *you* must be perceived as top dog and the one that makes the rules. It doesn't require yelling; it just requires control and the limiting of freedom.

1. Instead of turning your dog out on the entire property or yard when you leave, build a nice dog run and use it.
2. When you walk your dog, do not let him roam ahead, sniff at will and own the sidewalk. Limit his acceptable space to that beside or behind you. If you need help with pulling, consult with a good trainer. (I know one!)
3. At home with your dog, do not allow him to leave the room you are in. (He can't chew up your daughter's shoes if he can't sneak off to her closet.) Something as simple as this sends a powerful message to the dog.

Limit your dog's freedom and maximize your own control. It will fundamentally change your relationship with your dog. Love him, but control him.

Guarding

Dogs are protectors of their territory and property. That's what dogs are, and that is why we domesticated them to help us in the first place. Challenging dogs when they exhibit guarding behavior only provokes and intensifies their instinct to guard. You must, instead, address guarding at its source. You must also seek the help of a qualified professional in your area. *Do not try to fix this on your own!*

Guarding is related to status. A dog of high status in the group assumes he has the right *and duty* to guard whatever he determines is his property. Guarding behavior is disciplinary in nature. Dogs that guard things are doing so because they think it's their right and their duty to do so, and they are *disciplining* others who dare challenge this right. *The real cure for an overly guard-y dog is to change his perception of his status in your family.* Good obedience training and follow-through can do that.

But what if your dog continues to guard—his property, his things, etc.? Let's take them one at a time.

Guarding Territory

The dog that guards his territory probably has too much unrestricted freedom. A dog that is left free to roam his yard or property unrestricted and unsupervised, is a dog that fancies himself the king (or queen, as the case may be) of all he surveys.

1. Confine this dog when you are not present to supervise and control his freedom. He needs to know that he is a *guest* on your property—not the lord of the manor! A good and spacious dog run can work miracles for the dog that needs to be politely taken off his pedestal.
2. Allow him freedom to run the yard or property *only* when you are present to oversee. Disallow any guard-y or bark-y behavior by sweetly redirecting it. If necessary, he is allowed out of his dog run *only* on a "ball and chain"—meaning, with a long leash attached and dragging. This can do wonders in taking the starch out of a bossy dog's pantaloons.

Guarding Resources (Toys, Food, or Even *You*)

The dog that guards resources has been led to believe that he is top dog in the household or pack. In nature, the Alpha or top dog has ownership rights over everything. There is no sharing in nature! If you see your dog guarding his food or toys or bed...it's a pretty sure bet your dog sees himself in the Alpha position within your family, or at least in that situation.

1. Do *not* confront or punish your dog for this behavior. He will see this as a direct challenge to his position and he will defend his status with his teeth. Don't fight that battle unless you want a trip to the emergency room.

2. Enroll in a leadership-based obedience class. Learn how to cleverly yet clearly gain control over your dog without confrontation. Look for a class that teaches you how to set boundaries, disallow unwanted behaviors, and avoid confrontation while setting rules and enforcing standards of acceptable behavior without yelling or punishment.

3. Crate train your dog. Teach him that you are the keeper of the keys to freedom and the queen of the castle. His freedom within your household will be dependent upon you. This gives *you* both implied and direct power. It's a good position to be in.

4. Remove all high-value items from your household. If your dog guards rawhide chews, remove them from the premise. Why invite confrontation? Other, less exciting chew toys may be fine. You control what resources exist in the first place.

5. Keep a leash on your dog while you are supervising him. If he begins to guard items or resources, simply pick up the end of his leash and walk him out of the room. Sweetly put him into his crate or kennel with a small, edible treat reward. Shut the door.

6. Over time, you will gradually reclaim all power and status from your dog, without confronting or humiliating him in a public display. Once he finds himself in a position of lowered power and status, he will be less likely to guard and possess resources, since from his lowered status, this is no longer his to do.

Leash Aggression

I work a lot with leash aggression. In fact, it is the number one problem on which I consult. Virtually eight out of ten dog owners who seek my professional advice are concerned with leash aggression. It's a huge issue. If you are experiencing problems with leash aggression, please find a professional trainer in your area familiar with this behavior and work with him or her.

Generally, I find leash aggression rooted in fear and uncertainty, as opposed to true dominance. When a dog is on leash, he cannot exercise the most basic of instincts in the face of perceived danger: *to fight or flee.* The leash prevents the "flee," so the only option left for the nervous dog is to "fight."

In the majority of leash aggression cases, I find that simply keeping the dog in a specific, defined space at the owner's side, clarifying who's in charge and making the dog feel that someone has his back, improves or resolves most leash aggression issues. As trust increases, nervousness and fear are reduced and hence, the resulting aggression. Here is my standard advice:

1. Use the most effective training collar for your dog.
2. Walk your dog "in the office," at your side, insisting that he keep his front toes behind your toes, and that he stop when you stop. *Do not allow* walking ahead, sniffing the ground, or obsessive staring at other dogs. Snap the leash back crisply if the dog tries to walk ahead; otherwise, the leash must remain slack.
3. Block any "eye stalking" (an intense, unblinking stare-down) with my Fight Not Fan®, a piece of cardboard, your hand or other vision-blocking material. *DO NOT GIVE A HARSH LEASH CORRECTION* if your dog is already in eye-stalk mode! (Your dog may think it comes from the other dog and react even more aggressively.) An aggressive lunge is always preceded by this eye-stalk stare, so *if you block the stare, you virtually short-circuit the lunge.* Your vision blocker does this for you.

DOG "PICKS HIS VICTIM" BEFORE HE BEGINS EYE STALKING.

Fight Not Fan BLOCKS THE EYE STALKING.

Fight Not Fan CAN ALSO BE USED WHILE PASSING OTHER DOGS.

4. Remain as calm as possible as you enforce the rules of the Leadership Walk.
5. If your dog starts acting aggressively, sing a happy song and *keep walking* until you get out of Dodge. I'm serious. Singing can defuse a tense situation!

Fish and Other Dogs: THE LIMITS OF SOCIALIZATION

My husband hates fish. I wish he liked fish. I like fish. Don't all normal, healthy people like fish? Maybe if I put fish on his plate every night for dinner, fed him *more* fish, got him used to fish, surrounded him with fish...he'd learn to like fish. He just needs more *exposure* to fish.

How ridiculous is that reasoning? *But it's exactly what we do with our dogs when they do not like or act politely around other dogs. We think "more socialization" will fix it.*

Some people just don't enjoy fish, and *some dogs just don't enjoy other dogs.* So why do we keep trying to force them? Bringing a dog that doesn't like other dogs to a dog park "so he'll get socialized and learn to like other dogs" is like me serving fish for dinner every night to a husband who's been telling me for years that he *doesn't want, like or need* fish. My husband is happier with a salad and steak than fish, and many dogs are happier with *you* than with other dogs. Now, is that so bad?

Socialization is great and I highly recommend it, but it cannot transform a dog-averse canine into the social chairman of the dog park, any more than fish seven days a week will transform my husband into the Gorton's Fisherman.

Give it the old college try, then let your dog be that which Nature says he is.

Housetraining Issues

Some dogs housetrain themselves; others need our help in being convinced that it is more pleasant to do their business outside than on our Persian carpet.

For a dog, pooping and peeing is just another behavior, like begging at the table or hanging around the horses. Like with any behavior, he will repeat it if it ends in a good result and avoid it *only* if it ends in a less than pleasant result. If you feed your dog table scraps when he begs at the table, he will continue to beg. If one of the horses on the farm kicks out, he will avoid that horse in the future.

Some puppies are born with a fastidious nature. These are the puppies that find pooping and peeing in the house distasteful—because they don't like the smelly result. Voila! You have a puppy who asks to go outside when he needs to relieve himself and can be trusted to hold it all day until you return to let him out.

Other puppies aren't so prissy. They find the immediate relief from using your floor as a toilet to be gratifying, comfortable and worth repeating. They find more pleasure in the relief than they find displeasure in the stink. So how do you housetrain a puppy that doesn't care? You help him to care. Housetraining means a dog will actively work to avoid messing in the house, whether or not you are there to let him out. *Taking him outside every hour does not housetrain him!*

Like with any other behavior that you want your dog to avoid, you will need to *make* messing in the house *less* pleasant for the puppy. Only when a dog finds a behavior unpleasant from his perspective will he stop or avoid it. Just because *you* consider piles of stinky dog poop on your floor offensive doesn't mean your puppy feels the same. If he did, he'd be asking to go outside. From your dog's perspective, putting it there felt *good!* You need to change that.

1. First, crate train your puppy. You can use either a solid-style crate or a more open, wire model. Both will teach your dog to accept being confined to his own space. Because dogs are naturally "den" animals, puppies take readily to being crated and soon even seek out their crates for resting and quiet time. Crate training will be an important element in your housetraining program now, and in managing your dog in other ways later on. *Never use the crate as punishment.* Instead, think of it as a playpen in which you can put your puppy for up to four to five hours when you cannot supervise him. A crate-trained dog is a dog that's easy to live with.

A SOLID-STYLE CRATE

A WIRE CRATE

2. While he is crated, your puppy cannot mess on your floors, so you can take a shower, read a book or go to the store without worrying about what you'll find later.

3. When your puppy is out of his crate, he should have a leash dragging from his flat collar and you need to *watch his every move*. Never take your eyes off of him. If you need to focus on something else, put your puppy back in his crate. When he attempts to piddle or poop indoors, *carefully lob a penny can*. (See the Chapter 9 section: Don't-Do-That "Barks".) *Have the can land where he is doing his business*. He will think the carpet barked at him! You have just made the result of pooping or peeing inside the house "unpleasant." You're halfway there!

4. You quickly "rescue" your little one by taking his leash and walking him outside to an acceptable potty area. Praise him softly if he finishes his business. You have made it *more pleasant* to be outside when Nature calls.

5. Crate your puppy for up to four hours at a time, as well as overnight. You can have a life, your puppy will develop the ability to "hold it," and if you can catch and correct him "in the act," you'll be on your way to a well-housetrained dog!

6. You'll know that you have successfully housetrained your dog when he begins to whine or stand by the door when he needs to "go." You can then try leaving him alone in the house for increasing periods of time, from just thirty minutes to several hours. The naturally fastidious dog will handle that time alone responsibly. You can eventually be gone up to eight hours or more with that kind of dog. The dogs that don't care, however...probably best to crate them or let them hang out in a dog run if you have to leave for any considerable length of time. If you are not there to open the door, they tend to exercise option B—*going on the carpet*.

Counter-Surfing

Dogs are hunters and scavengers. An unsupervised dog will do what his DNA tells him to do—indoors or out. As with everything involving dogs, the key is disallowing counter-surfing when you are with him, and conditioning for avoidance when you are out of the room.

Do not leave food on your counter and your dog unsupervised. You are asking for trouble. Of course, he will find the food and scavenge it. To him, this is not wrong; it is natural behavior. To train your dog to avoid the temptation of food left on the counter or table, set up a "teaching moment."

1. Intentionally leave something yummy on the counter or table.
2. Hide somewhere just out of the room, with a training can in your hand, at the ready.
3. When your dog approaches the counter and lifts his nose in a sniffing motion as he assesses the prize above, toss the training can quickly and noisily under his feet, letting it crash against the baseboard of the counter. Wow! The dog will jump back, thinking once again that the barking trolls are guarding the counter tops.
4. You rush in and "rescue" your dog, petting and telling him that the trolls are indeed a scary lot, but that if he just sticks by you, you will watch over him and guarantee his safety and well being.

Done. No more counter-surfing.

Keep Away/Catch Me

This is a game of challenge. If your dog is engaging you in a game of keep away or catch-me-if-you-can, he is testing your authority. He is goading you into a contest to determine who controls whom. *Do not take the bait!* You cannot win the contest he is waging. Your dog is faster and quicker than you can ever be. If you accept his challenge, you have already lost. If you lose, you also lose your status as leader. If you are not your dog's leader, you cannot control his behavior. It is a slippery slope and a dangerous vortex, like Alice down the rabbit hole.

When your dog challenges you to a game of Keep Away or Catch Me:

1. Stand still. Your dog will be confused. You're not playing the game. Why are you not chasing him? As in life, refuse to be baited.

2. Calmly ask him to "Stay," and take one step forward. Stand still until he stops moving.

3. Repeat your "Stay" command, and when the dog stops moving away, take that next step forward. You are winning.

4. Eventually, the dog will stop moving away, because the fun is gone from the game. You're not playing it, so he will stop as well. You will eventually get to your dog.

5. *Most importantly*, when you finally reach your dog, *do not yell or punish!* The result of him letting you reach him must be a good one. Pet him softly, put on his leash and walk him back to the house or car or wherever you want him to be. If he has something in his mouth, let him keep whatever he has for the time being. Be nonchalant. That is your power.

6. Now *trade* him what he has (Barbie, socks, a spare-rib) for something else equally attractive to him. Offer him a cookie, a ball, a squeaky toy or something else worth having. Act like it doesn't matter to you either way. It's the art of negotiation. If you make him think what he has is valuable to you, he will lock on and not release it. He's like the little boy in the sandbox who doesn't give his pail and shovel much thought until another little boy tries to take them away. Then, they're the most valuable toys in the sandbox—and they are *his*.

7. Remember, your dog is all about results. Giving something up to *you* must result in something good for *him*, or he's not going to cooperate. He's just a dog.

In Closing

Dogs can teach us much—about ourselves, about others and about the world. We all have self-interests, egos, and seek pleasant results in our lives. Leadership is about focus and control, not confrontation or aggression. Nature teaches us that we can get what we want by influencing the behaviors of others through the clever use of pleasant feedback and results, instead of bullying or force. I hope that **Lipstick and the Leash** will encourage, empower and enable women (and men) everywhere to achieve all that they desire, and to be all that they are capable of being. It has been my pleasure to share it with you.

Good luck to all of you, my friends. In Dogs We Trust.

❖ Appendix ❖

Essential Tools for Dog-Training Success

Your Essential Dog Training Tools

Here is my list of essential tools for dog training success. Some of these items can be found at your local pet supply retailer. Others are available only through my on-line store:
www.dogtalkstore.com

The Basics

- **6' Cotton or Leather Leash**
- **4'-6' Chew-Proof Tether**
  To temporarily keep your dog in one spot while you are home with him but too busy to watch with an eagle-eye.
- **30' Long Line**
  My "Coming Mother!" cord can be used for so many things, from teaching a dependable Come command to helping your puppy learn to stay in the same room with you.
- **Training Collar**
  You will need to choose the correct training collar for your dog. The "correct" collar is the one that can effectively teach him that he is not allowed to walk ahead of you! See Chapter 9: **Learn to Speak Dog.**
- **6"-8" Indoor Collar Tab**
  My "What Did Mama Say?" tab is your "instant leash" and attaches to your dog's collar while he is indoors with you. It helps you follow-through on all commands. Chew-resistant.
- **A Set of my Training Cans**
  An absolute "must" for teaching a dog not to jump up, solving housebreaking issues and more. Training cans make off-leash control in the home possible!

- **Treat Pouch**
  Be prepared to "thank" your dog for doing what you ask – especially coming when called. Do not use treats as bribery; use them as rewards for doing things your way.
- **Crate**
  For dogs left alone indoors up to 5 hours.
- **Outdoor Dog Run**
  For medium to large dogs left alone more than 5 hours at a time.

Other Useful Tools

- **Don't Do That! Concentrate**
  Dilute with water and use in your own spray bottle at home. My formula includes citronella which is distasteful to the dog and can help stop all sorts of unwanted behaviors!
- **Citronella Bark Collar**
  This collar emits a sudden burst of citronella mist whenever the dog barks and is my favorite tool for stopping nuisance barking when I am not at home.
- **Fight-Not Fan**
  My own invention for controlling leash aggression. Carry it on your walks and "block" any challenging eye contact between your dog and another. Very effective!
- **Alert Scarf**
  – Worn by your dog, caution-yellow Alert Scarves politely tell others that he or she should not be approached. Available in these wording choices:
  - SHY DOG: Don't Rush Up
  - IN TRAINING: Please Don't Pet
  - NO DOGS: I'm socially challenged

The Author, Camilla Gray-Nelson

I was born on a dairy farm in Petaluma, CA. While other little girls my age were playing with their friends and having tea parties with their dolls, I was catching cows to ride, figuring out how to gather eggs without being pecked by the hens, and teaching my ponies tricks. In fact, most of my friends growing up had four legs, not two.

My brothers and I weren't micro-managed as children, but we knew without a doubt that our parents were in charge of our family – just like the cows, horses and dogs also knew who set the rules in their own herds or packs. My parents did not yell; they simply set and enforced the rules – like the lead horse, the queen cow and the alpha dog did in their own groups. From my earliest days on the farm I learned a great truth: the secret to getting what you want and influencing others is quiet strength, feedback and follow-through, not yelling, bribery or conflict. Nature taught me this. My parents proved it. I live it.

When I started training dogs professionally, it was women who sought out my help. Responsibility for the family dog typically falls to them, after all. Their homes were in chaos. They were yelling at their dogs (and their kids) but could not control either one. The life skills of personal power that I learned as a child turned out to be rare among my clients. Since that time, I have been on a mission to empower women (and men), not only with their dogs, but in their greater lives as well – by sharing Nature's secrets of quiet strength and influence.

Unleash your Inner Leader!

Made in the USA
Middletown, DE
19 February 2022

61486573R00119